16

DEAD

MEN

16
DEAD
MEN

THE EASTER RISING EXECUTIONS

ANNE-MARIE RYAN

MERCIER PRESS

Irish Publisher – Irish Story

For my parents,
Kevin and Mary Ryan

Sixteen Dead Men

O but we talked at large before
The sixteen men were shot,
But who can talk of give and take,
What should be and what not
While those dead men are loitering there
To stir the boiling pot?

You say that we should still the land
Till Germany's overcome;
But who is there to argue that
Now Pearse is deaf and dumb?
And is their logic to outweigh
MacDonagh's bony thumb?

How could you dream they'd listen
That have an ear alone
For those new comrades they have found,
Lord Edward and Wolfe Tone,
Or meddle with our give and take
That converse bone to bone?

W. B. Yeats

MERCIER PRESS

Cork

www.mercierpress.ie

© Anne-Marie Ryan, 2014

ISBN: 978 1 78117 134 9

10 9 8 7 6 5 4 3 2 1

A CIP record for this title is available from the British Library

Printed and bound in the EU.

CONTENTS

Abbreviations

AOH	Ancient Order of Hibernians
BMH	Bureau of Military History
CYMS	Catholic Young Men's Society
DMP	Dublin Metropolitan Police
GAA	Gaelic Athletic Association
GPO	General Post Office
GSWR	Great Southern and Western Railway
ICA	Irish Citizen Army
ILP	Independent Labour Party of Ireland
IRA	Irish Republican Army
IRB	Irish Republican Brotherhood
ISRP	Irish Socialist Republican Party
ITGWU	Irish Transport and General Workers' Union
IWW	International Workers of the World
NAI	National Archives of Ireland
NLI	National Library of Ireland
RIC	Royal Irish Constabulary
SPI	Socialist Party of Ireland
SSF	Scottish Socialist Federation
UCD	University College Dublin
UVF	Ulster Volunteer Force

ACKNOWLEDGEMENTS

I am grateful for the support of a number of individuals and institutions while researching and writing this book.

The staff of the reading room at the National Library of Ireland went out of their way on many occasions to locate material. I am also grateful to the staff of the libraries of University College Dublin and Trinity College Dublin. The Trojan work of the staff of the Military Archives in digitising the witness statements collected by the Bureau of Military History between 1947 and 1957 has been of enormous assistance in preparing this book.

I would like to thank the staff at Mercier Press, in particular Mary Feehan and Wendy Logue, for their assistance and encouragement throughout the production of this book. I would also like to thank Robert Doran for his work on proofreading the text.

I acknowledge the support of my former colleagues at Kilmainham Gaol Museum, who over the years have been a source of information, debate and inspiration. I am grateful for the assistance of Niall Bergin, who provided images from the Kilmainham Gaol collection for this book. I would like to give particular thanks to Brian Crowley, curator of the Pearse Museum, for the mentoring, advice and help he gave me throughout my time working for the Office of Public Works.

This book would not have been possible without the patience and encouragement of my family and friends, too numerous to mention here by name.

I owe an eternal debt of gratitude to my parents, Kevin and Mary Ryan, to whom this book is dedicated.

INTRODUCTION

The 'Sixteen Dead Men' about whom Yeats wrote his poem in the aftermath of the Easter Rising were a diverse group. Ranging in age from twenty-five to fifty-eight, their occupations included headmaster, tobacconist, poet, railway clerk, university lecturer, printer, humanitarian, water bailiff, art teacher, silk weaver, corporation clerk, farmer, trade union leader, bookkeeper, chemist's clerk and newspaper manager. Two of the leaders were born outside Ireland: Thomas Clarke in the unlikely location of a British Army barracks on the Isle of Wight, James Connolly in the Irish ghetto of Edinburgh. Some had complicated national and religious identities: Patrick and Willie Pearse were the sons of an English stone carver, Thomas MacDonagh's mother was the daughter of English parents, Roger Casement was raised a Protestant but secretly baptised a Catholic by his mother, and John MacBride was the son of an Ulster-Scots Protestant from Co. Antrim. Others had close links with the institutions of British imperialism that they would later fight against: Michael Mallin and James Connolly were former soldiers in the British Army, Éamonn Ceannt was the son of a Royal Irish Constabulary (RIC) constable and Roger Casement had been knighted for his services as a British consul exposing the dark side of the rubber trade in the Congo and Peru.

This group of men, who participated in an armed rebellion against British rule in Ireland in April 1916, came to the point of insurrection by a variety of pathways. For many of them, their revolutionary instinct had developed at a young age. Thomas Kent was in his early twenties when he was imprisoned for his activities with the Land League in Co. Cork in the late nineteenth century, Michael O'Hanrahan grew up hearing stories of his ancestors' involvement in the 1798 rebellion in Co. Wexford, Edward Daly was born into a Limerick family prominent in the Fenian movement, Con Colbert and Seán Heuston were members of the nationalist youth organisation Na Fianna Éireann, and Seán Mac Diarmada's republican politics were nurtured by his national schoolteacher, who provided him with books on Irish history.

For some, the declaration of an Irish Republic on 24 April 1916 was the culmination of a lifetime's struggle. Thomas Clarke had become active in the secret revolutionary organisation the Irish Republican Brotherhood (IRB) as a young man and had served fifteen years' imprisonment for his involvement in the preparations for a Fenian bombing campaign in Britain; James Connolly had devoted his adult life to improving conditions for working-class people in Scotland, Ireland and America, and was a long-standing advocate of the establishment of a socialist Irish republic. But for others, the conversion to radical nationalism came late. Patrick Pearse was a speaker at a pro-Home Rule rally as late as March 1912, Éamonn Ceannt's nationalist activities were mostly confined to the Irish language movement until he was elected to the Provisional Committee of the Irish Volunteers in November 1913, while Thomas MacDonagh was not co-opted onto the Supreme Council of the IRB until shortly before the Easter Rising.

Seven of the executed leaders of the rebellion sealed their fate by signing the Proclamation of the Irish Republic shortly before the outbreak of the Rising. The document, which declared 'the right of the Irish people to the ownership of Ireland' and which guaranteed 'religious and civil liberty, equal rights and equal opportunities to all its citizens', was read aloud by Patrick Pearse outside the General Post Office (GPO) on Sackville Street (now O'Connell Street) shortly after noon on Easter Monday. Pearse was president of the provisional government and commander-in-chief of the army of the Irish Republic. He was accompanied by Thomas Clarke, the mastermind of the rebellion, who was invited to be the first signatory of the Proclamation in deference to his contribution to the Fenian movement since the late 1870s. Also present was James Connolly, a fellow signatory and commandant-general of the forces of the Irish Republic in Dublin. Two other signatories were also stationed in the GPO, the headquarters of the rebel forces: Joseph Plunkett, the military strategist of the rebellion, who was dying from tuberculosis, and Seán Mac Diarmada, Clarke's right-hand man, whose involvement in the action was restricted by lameness in his right leg caused by a bout of polio. The remaining two signatories were in command of outposts in the south-west of Dublin city. Thomas MacDonagh, commandant of the 2nd Battalion, Dublin Brigade of the Irish Volunteers, saw relatively little action at his position at Jacob's biscuit factory on Bishop Street. By contrast, Éamonn Ceannt, commandant of the 4th Battalion, was involved in intense fighting during Easter Week at the South Dublin Union, a workhouse and hospital complex in the Rialto area of the city.

For the other executed men, the extent of their involvement in the planning of the uprising and their participation in it varied greatly. Edward Daly, like MacDonagh and Ceannt, held the position of commandant of a Volunteer battalion, but he did not learn of the plans for the Easter Rising until the Wednesday before it was due to take place. His rank as commandant of the 1st Battalion, positioned in the area surrounding the Four Courts, ensured that his death sentence was carried out. Likewise Michael Mallin, who held the rank of commandant in Connolly's Irish Citizen Army (ICA), faced the firing squad for his role in leading the rebel forces who seized the Royal College of Surgeons on St Stephen's Green during Easter Week.

John MacBride was a veteran Fenian, but his alcoholism and humiliating divorce from Maud Gonne made him an outcast in republican circles and he was not involved in the planning of the Rising. His chance encounter with Irish Volunteers as they assembled at St Stephen's Green on Easter Monday, while he was on his way to his brother's wedding, led to his appointment by Thomas MacDonagh as second-in-command at Jacob's. MacBride's accidental participation in the rebellion, along with the British authorities' longstanding resentment of his organisation of the Irish Brigade that fought against the British during the Boer War in South Africa, led to his execution in the Stonebreakers' Yard of Kilmainham Gaol. Michael O'Hanrahan, who fought alongside MacBride in Jacob's, held only the rank of quartermaster of the 2nd Battalion. His execution may have owed much to the fact that he was known to the police as a clerk working in the offices of the Irish Volunteers, but it is equally likely that it was due to the fact he was sentenced to death early on in the period of executions, before the tide of public opinion turned against the authorities. Similarly Con Colbert and Seán Heuston – who commanded smaller outposts at Jameson's Distillery in Marrowbone Lane and the Mendicity Institution – were both executed on 8 May 1916, three days before John Dillon addressed the House of Commons and accused the British authorities of 'letting loose a river of blood' in their response to the uprising.

Willie Pearse's participation in the Easter Rising came about entirely through his close relationship with his brother, Patrick. He was involved in the planning of it only insofar as he accompanied his brother to meetings, and throughout the rebellion he mostly acted as aide-de-camp to the newly appointed president of the Irish Republic in the GPO. Unique among the executed rebels, he pleaded guilty to the charge that he 'did an act to wit take part in an armed rebellion and in the waging of war against His Majesty the King'. His guilty plea may have bolstered the case for his execution, but he certainly did not play a significant leadership role in the Rising, and his execution can be linked to the fact that he was the brother of the commandant of the rebels.

All fourteen rebels who were executed as a result of their participation in the Easter Rising in Dublin were shot in the Stonebreakers' Yard at Kilmainham Gaol. Elsewhere, Thomas Kent faced a firing squad at Cork Detention Barracks and Roger Casement was hanged at Pentonville Prison in London. Although Kent faced the same charge as the Dublin men – participating in an armed rebellion – he was not a leader of the Easter Rising and there was little or no rebel activity in Co. Cork in April 1916. His execution was the result of a military raid on the Kent family home at Bawnard, during which a member of the RIC was fatally wounded. Roger Casement's involvement in the Easter Rising was over before the rebellion had even started. Casement had been working in Germany to raise support for a rebellion in Ireland and was arrested on Banna Strand, Co. Kerry on Good Friday 1916, after an attempt to land arms for the rebellion failed. His hanging at Pentonville on 3 August 1916 brought to an end the executions of those involved in the Easter Rising.

The rebellion, which started in Dublin on 24 April 1916, was the outcome of a series of events that had begun with the introduction of a Home Rule Bill in the House of Commons on 11 April 1912 by the British prime minister,

Herbert Asquith. This was the third attempt to legislate for self-government for Ireland since 1886. However, this time it appeared the efforts of the Liberal Party and their allies in government, the Irish Parliamentary Party, would be successful. The House of Lords had lost its power of veto on bills from the House of Commons in August 1911, and now the way was clear for the enactment of the Home Rule Bill within two years of its passing. The proposed introduction of Home Rule prompted strong opposition in parts of Ulster, with protests concentrated in the four counties in the north-east of the province. The majority unionist, Protestant population there was outraged by what they perceived as a threat to the union of Great Britain and Ireland. On 28 September 1912, Ulster Day, half a million people signed the Ulster Solemn League and Covenant, pledging to oppose the introduction of Home Rule. By the end of the year a volunteer militia, the Ulster Volunteer Force (UVF), had formed to oppose Home Rule, by force if necessary.

The formation of the UVF prompted nationalists in the south of Ireland to imitate the Ulster unionists by setting up their own military force. The Irish Volunteers were founded at a meeting at the Rotunda Rink in Dublin on 25 November 1913. Unlike the UVF, however, their aim was to defend the introduction of Home Rule in Ireland.

The year 1913 had been an eventful one, particularly in Dublin. In August 1913 William Martin Murphy, a major Dublin employer, instigated an industrial dispute when he 'locked out' from their jobs employees who were members of the Irish Transport and General Workers' Union (ITGWU). The subsequent strike, led by James Larkin and James Connolly, lasted until early 1914, during which time another volunteer militia, the ICA, was formed to protect the interests of workers.

Tensions were heightened in 1914 as the deadline for implementing Home Rule approached. In April 1914 the UVF landed arms at Larne, an event largely ignored by the authorities. The Irish Volunteers staged their own gun-runnings in July and August 1914 at Howth in Co. Dublin and Kilcoole in Co. Wicklow. Soldiers of the King's Own Scottish Borderers, returning to Dublin city centre after their efforts to prevent the landing of arms at Howth had failed, opened fire when a crowd on Bachelor's Walk began to jeer them. They killed four civilians.

But the event that changed the course of history, and which made the Easter Rising possible, was the outbreak of war in Europe in August 1914. The immediate consequence for Ireland was the suspension of the implementation of Home Rule until after the war. On 20 September 1914 John Redmond, the leader of the Irish Parliamentary Party, made a speech at Woodenbridge in Co. Wicklow in which he encouraged members of the Irish Volunteers to join the British Army, in anticipation that Ireland would be rewarded with Home Rule at the end of the war. This prompted a split in the Irish Volunteers and the vast majority of the estimated

188,000 members followed Redmond and joined a new organisation, the National Volunteers. The remaining men, at most 13,500, stayed with the Irish Volunteers and were led by Eoin MacNeill.

The Irish Volunteers formed the nucleus of the men who would participate in the Easter Rising. At a meeting of key figures in the nationalist movement at the library of the Gaelic League on 9 September 1914, it was decided in principle to stage a rebellion against British rule while the war in Europe was ongoing. The old republican dictum 'England's difficulty is Ireland's opportunity' became the mantra of radical Irish nationalists, including Thomas Clarke, who had long regretted the failure to have an uprising in Ireland during the Boer War, when the British Army was engaged in southern Africa. The planning of the rebellion was carried out by the secret oath-bound organisation, the IRB. Clarke and Mac Diarmada directed the course of events, rejuvenating the IRB with younger members, infiltrating other nationalist organisations such as the Gaelic Athletic Association (GAA), seeking financial assistance from republican figures in the United States and building a network of like-minded individuals around Ireland. An IRB military committee was formed. Its membership initially included only Pearse, Plunkett and Ceannt, but it was eventually expanded to include Clarke and Mac Diarmada.

By January 1916 preparations for a rising were under way. At this point senior IRB members became concerned that James Connolly, commander of the ICA, was planning on staging his own socialist uprising. Knowing that a small ICA rebellion would scupper plans for their larger rebellion, IRB leaders confronted Connolly. They persuaded him to hold back on his plans for an uprising, and Easter Sunday 1916 was agreed as the date for a joint ICA/Irish Volunteers rebellion.

Not everyone in the republican movement approved of a rebellion, however, not least Eoin MacNeill, president of the Irish Volunteers, and senior IRB figures Bulmer Hobson and Michael O'Rahilly. These men believed an uprising should only occur if there was a strong possibility of success or if the Volunteers were attacked first by the British. MacNeill was kept in the dark and did not learn of plans for the rebellion until the Thursday before Easter Sunday. When he heard on Holy Saturday of the sinking of a German ship carrying arms for the Volunteers off the coast of Co. Kerry, MacNeill decided he should stop the rebellion. Late that evening he issued a countermanding order, published in the *Sunday Independent*, cancelling all Volunteer manoeuvres for Easter Sunday. Chaos ensued, but at a meeting of the Supreme Council of the IRB at Dublin's Liberty Hall on Easter Sunday, it was decided that the rebellion would take place the next day.

On the morning of Easter Monday, approximately 1,000 men and women seized control of important buildings across Dublin city, taking the GPO as their headquarters. The Irish Volunteers made up the largest proportion of the rebels and were reinforced by the ICA. It is estimated that 140 women were active participants in the Rising.[1] Female members of the

ICA were involved in the fighting, while members of Cumann na mBan, the female auxiliary force of the Irish Volunteers, participated by mostly acting as couriers, tending to the wounded and cooking meals for the rebel garrisons.

The effort to hold City Hall was over by Tuesday, but the rebels held on to most of their positions until the evacuation of the GPO on Friday. Overwhelmed by the strength of the British forces and seeking to prevent further civilian casualties, Pearse surrendered to Brigadier General W. H. M. Lowe at 2.30 p.m. on Saturday 29 April. The vast majority of the rebels were brought to Richmond Barracks, where the leaders were identified and court-martialled. Those considered to be ordinary rebels were transferred to Frongoch internment camp in Wales. In total, 186 men and one woman were tried by court martial in the aftermath of the Easter Rising.[2] The death sentence was confirmed in fifteen cases and those who were spared execution were imprisoned in England.

The stories of the sixteen men executed following the Easter Rising are not, of course, the story of the entire rebellion. Other figures on the rebel side also played significant leadership roles. Éamon de Valera, commandant of the 3rd Battalion Dublin Brigade of the Irish Volunteers at Boland's Mills, was sentenced to death. He avoided execution, possibly because he held American citizenship but more likely because he was not court-martialled until 8 May, by which point the British authorities had decided to execute only the most prominent rebel leaders. Constance Markievicz, second-in-command at

St Stephen's Green, was also sentenced to death but spared the firing squad: the execution of a woman would have outraged public opinion. Other prominent rebels were killed in action, including Michael O'Rahilly, shot dead on Moore Street in the retreat from the GPO, Seán Connolly, who led the attack on City Hall and was killed there, and Michael Malone, who was in command at Mount Street Bridge during an attack on British reinforcements marching in from Kingstown (Dún Laoghaire).

In total, sixty-four rebels died in action during Easter Week and sixteen were executed. There were 132 casualties in the British Army and Dublin Metropolitan Police (DMP) and 230 civilians died as a result of the fighting. It is the stories of the men and women who participated in the rebellion, who witnessed it happening or who tried to suppress it, that make up the narrative of the Easter Rising. But the 'Sixteen Dead Men' who were executed for their part in the rebellion became the martyrs of Easter Week and provided the inspiration for the subsequent revolution in Ireland. Their stories did, as Yeats wrote, 'stir the boiling pot'.

PATRICK PEARSE

There was little in Patrick Pearse's childhood and upbringing to suggest that one day he would command a rebellion against British rule in Ireland. The son of an English father and an Irish mother, he was born on 10 November 1879 at 27 Great Brunswick Street, Dublin, the location of the Pearse family home and stone-carving business.

His father, James, was born in Bloomsbury, London, and trained as a stone sculptor in Birmingham. He came to Ireland, possibly in the late 1850s or early 1860s, to take advantage of a boom in church building.[1] James Pearse was a self-educated man who read widely on various topics and was most likely an atheist. In 1886 he published a pamphlet in support of Home Rule.

Patrick's mother, Margaret (née Brady), came from a farming background in Co. Meath; her father later worked in the coal business at the North Strand in Dublin. Her grandfather and great-uncle are believed to have fought in the 1798 rebellion. Margaret was James's second wife. His first wife, Emily (née Fox), died in 1876. Patrick had a step-brother and step-sister from his father's first marriage, and an older sister (Margaret), a younger brother (William) and younger sister (Mary Brighid). Pearse was conscious of the diverse backgrounds of his parents and of the influence they had on his development. He later wrote in his unfinished autobiography:

> [W]hen my father and my mother married there came together two widely remote traditions – English and Puritan and mechanic on one hand, Gaelic and Catholic and peasant on the other; freedom loving both, and neither without its strain of poetry and its experience of spiritual and other adventure. And these two proper traditions worked in me and, fused together by a certain fire proper to myself … made me the strange thing I am.[2]

Although he lived for most of his childhood in close proximity to the tenement dwellings of Dublin's poor at Townsend

Street, Pearse's upbringing was mostly comfortable, as his father's business prospered. His early childhood was spent in the company of his siblings and cousins, playing with their wooden horse, Dobbin, riding the circular tramline from Westland Row to College Green and later using the magic lantern his father bought him to give slideshow lectures to his family.[3] He attended the Christian Brothers school on Westland Row, where he stood out from the other children because of his slight English accent.[4] Pearse was a diligent student and it was at Westland Row that he began learning Irish under the tutelage of Brother Maunsell, a native speaker from Co. Kerry. He completed the Intermediate Certificate examinations in 1896, coming second in the country in the Irish exam. At seventeen years of age, he was too young to begin his studies at the Royal University and in the intervening period he taught Irish at Westland Row and founded the New Ireland Literary Society, where members gave lectures on literary topics. In 1898 he began his studies for a Bachelor of Arts degree at the Royal University and also studied for the bar exams at the King's Inns. Pearse qualified as a barrister in 1901 and never practised as a lawyer, although he did represent a Donegal poet, Niall Mac Ghiolla Bhríde, over his right to have his name painted in Irish on his cart.

The Gaelic League – an organisation founded in 1893 to promote and protect the Irish language – was the focus of Pearse's professional life in his early adulthood and his involvement made him known in Irish nationalist circles. He joined in 1896 and began attending meetings of the central branch. He quickly came to prominence, becoming a member of the Coiste Gnótha (executive committee) in autumn 1898 and was appointed secretary of the publications committee in June 1900. Pearse showed a level of dedication to the Gaelic League that he demonstrated for other, more political causes later in his life. He missed just six out of 109 meetings of the Coiste Gnótha during his first year as a member of the committee and as publications secretary he rapidly expanded the number of books and pamphlets produced by the Gaelic League.[5] The League provided Pearse with a ready-made social circle and he benefited from the travel opportunities presented by the organisation, including trips to Cardiff, Paris and Glasgow.

In March 1903 Pearse was elected editor of *An Claidheamh Soluis*, the weekly newspaper of the Gaelic League. His plans to expand the paper impressed those who voted for him, although, when implemented, his modernising efforts caused financial difficulties for the League. Pearse's contributions to the newspaper were non-political and often concerned issues relating to education, particularly the status of the Irish language in schools. A trip to Belgium in 1905, during which he visited schools to see bilingualism in practice and study the use of the Direct Method for teaching languages, provided him with extensive material for his editorials in *An Claidheamh*.

Pearse's devotion to the Irish language helped to foster in him a love of the West of Ireland, in particular the Gaeltacht region of Connemara. He learned the dialect of this area and spent his summers living among the native speakers at his summer house in Rosmuck, and he considered the West of Ireland to be the purest living example of an Irish-speaking, Gaelicised Ireland:

> In the kindly Irish west I feel that I am in Ireland. To feel so in Dublin, where my work lies, sometimes requires a more rigorous effort of imagination than I am capable of.[6]

The west also provided Pearse with the inspiration for his writings, including a collection of short stories, *Íosagán agus Sgéalta Eile*, published by the Gaelic League in 1907. However, Pearse had a tendency to romanticise life in the West of Ireland and ignore the poverty experienced by the people living there. He wrote articles in *An Claidheamh Soluis* opposing emigration from the west as it contributed to the decline of the language, but he failed to acknowledge the economic realities that forced people to leave their homes.

Pearse's research and writings on education eventually brought him to a decision to establish his own school for boys. Scoil Éanna, or St Enda's College, was to be different from any other school in Ireland at that time. The Irish language and culture would be at the heart of the school, new teaching practices – including the Direct Method and bilingual teaching – would be utilised, the curriculum would include modern subjects, including European languages, zoology, shorthand and book-keeping, and students would experience a holistic education with an emphasis on sport, drama and other activities. St Enda's opened at Cullenswood House, Ranelagh, in September 1908. Pupils included the sons of important members of the Gaelic League and the school had high-profile supporters, including Douglas Hyde, Eoin MacNeill, W. B. Yeats and Padraic Colum, all of whom gave lectures to the boys during the first school year. Kenneth Reddin, a former pupil of the school, summed up his sense of what made St Enda's different to other schools:

> The atmosphere of St Enda's was completely un-institutional. I have never looked into the Refectory of any great Public School and sensed its bareness and cleanliness without thinking of a prison, a reformatory, or a hospital. The atmosphere of St Enda's was neither that of a prison, a reformatory, nor a hospital. In fact at night we often went down to Mrs Pearse for a biscuit or, if that failed, for a slice of bread and a glass of milk, or to Miss Pearse or Miss Brady. ... And in the Refectory we all ate together, Headmaster, teachers and students. We lived en famille, and in full family atmosphere.[7]

In 1910 Pearse decided to relocate the school to a more rural setting in Rathfarnham, South Dublin, and he obtained a lease on a large house called the Hermitage, which was surrounded by extensive grounds. He also established a school for girls, Scoil Íde, at Cullenswood House. The move to Rathfarnham had disastrous consequences for the school, as Pearse could not afford to rent the Hermitage or pay for the expensive alterations required. Fewer day pupils attended because the school was too far from the transport network of the city centre. Pearse's financial difficulties continued until the end of his life.

Pearse was a shy person and was something of an outsider at social occasions. Some of his insecurity was brought about by the fact that he was self-conscious about a cast in his left eye. He always posed for photographs in profile so that the cast would not be seen. Pearse's closest friend was undoubtedly his brother, Willie, who taught art at St Enda's. Willie was Patrick's confidant and could influence his actions. Their mutual friend Desmond Ryan later wrote: 'Pearse listened most courteously to all critics and went on doing as he liked until Willie lisped his fierce word'.[8] Pearse never married, although he was linked romantically to Eveleen Nicholls, who drowned while swimming off the coast of Kerry in 1909. Although he had some close friendships with women – he holidayed in the West of Ireland with Mary Hayden, a colleague in the Gaelic League, seventeen years his senior – Pearse could behave quite awkwardly in female company.

Pearse first came under the influence of ideas around Irish independence when he moved his school to Rathfarnham in 1910. One of the reasons Pearse chose to relocate to the Hermitage was its association with one of the great heroes of Irish nationalism, Robert Emmet, who was executed for his leadership of a small rebellion in Dublin in 1803. Emmet was believed to have courted his love, Sarah Curran, in the grounds of the Hermitage, which was situated near her home. Shortly after the move to the Hermitage, Pearse began reading the writings of the republican leader Theobald Wolfe Tone and the *Jail Journal* of John Mitchel. Emmet, Tone and Mitchel greatly influenced the development of his nationalist thinking.

Pearse first came to prominence in advanced nationalist circles when he was asked by Seán Mac Diarmada to speak at a Robert Emmet commemoration in 1911. Mac Diarmada and his close associate Thomas Clarke were key figures in the IRB – the secret underground organisation responsible for the planning of the Easter Rising – and they were impressed by his speech.

However, up until 1912 Pearse's interest in politics was mostly confined to the Irish language and education policy. His development as an advanced nationalist came later. As late as March 1912 he spoke at a rally on Sackville Street, Dublin, in support of the Third Home Rule Bill, introduced to parliament by Prime Minister Herbert Asquith. Pearse spoke in favour of the prospect of limited self-government for Ireland, but warned that if the bill was not passed there would be war in Ireland.

Pearse felt that he needed an Irish language platform from which to express his developing political ideas and he founded a newspaper in 1912, *An Barr Buadh*, which ran for eleven issues. He also contributed articles to the radical newspaper *Irish Freedom*.

Pearse's growing involvement in Irish politics coincided

with an extraordinary period in Irish history during which new organisations were formed to try to determine the future of Ireland. The prospect of Home Rule was strongly resisted by the majority Protestant population in north-east Ulster. In September 1912 nearly half a million men and women signed the Ulster Solemn League and Covenant, pledging to defend the province from the introduction of Home Rule. Four months later 100,000 men who had signed the Covenant joined the UVF, a militia which aimed to resist Home Rule by force. The landing of arms by the UVF at Larne in April 1914 demonstrated that the organisation was serious in its intent.

Meanwhile, in Dublin nationalists began to suggest the formation of a similar organisation to protect Home Rule. In an article, 'The Coming Revolution', published in November 1913, Pearse wrote: 'I am glad that the Orangemen have armed, for it is a goodly thing to see arms in Irish hands. ... I should like to see any and every body of Irish citizens armed'.[9] That same month, Eoin MacNeill raised the prospect of forming a militia in the south in an article in *An Claidheamh Soluis*, entitled 'The North Began'. A meeting was held at Wynn's Hotel, Dublin, on 11 November 1913 to discuss the formation of a militia, and it is indicative of Pearse's growing importance in nationalist circles that he was invited to this meeting.

The Irish Volunteers was formally founded at a meeting on 25 November 1913 at Dublin's Rotunda Rink, where over 5,000 people were in attendance. Pearse spoke at the meeting and was made a member of the Provisional Committee and also held the position of director of organisation. The following month he was sworn into the IRB and his conversion to radical nationalist politics was almost complete.

The financial situation at St Enda's had reached crisis point by early 1914. Pearse decided to go on a lecture tour of the USA to raise funds for the school and he used his connections in the IRB to make contact with radical Irish-Americans John Devoy and Joseph McGarrity, who helped him to organise the tour. From February to May 1914 he travelled around cities in America delivering lectures on a variety of topics, most notably some fiery addresses on Robert Emmet. He raised $3,000, enough to keep St Enda's open until at least the following year. When he returned he threw himself into his work for the Irish Volunteers and IRB but was increasingly frustrated at meetings of the Provisional Committee, which had been restructured to include twenty-five members nominated by John Redmond, the leader of the Irish Parliamentary Party. So instead Pearse focused his attention on securing arms for the Volunteers, and in August 1914 he allowed St Enda's to be used as a storage facility for arms and ammunition landed during the gun-runnings at Howth and Kilcoole.

The outbreak of war between Britain and Germany in the same month precipitated a split in the Irish Volunteers. Redmond, in a speech at Woodenbridge, Co. Wicklow, on 20 September, called on the Irish Volunteers to join the British Army. Pearse and the other members of the original Provisional Committee of the Irish Volunteers rejected this proposal. They were in a minority – British intelligence estimated that 93 per cent of the 188,000-strong membership followed Redmond and his new organisation, the National Volunteers. In the drastically reduced Irish Volunteers, Pearse was made director of organisation of the military headquarters established in December 1914. He also moved upwards in the IRB: in May 1915 he was appointed director of military organisation on a three-man military committee tasked with planning a rising.

His rise to prominence in the nationalist movement reached its zenith in August 1915, when he was asked by Clarke to give the graveside oration at the funeral of the Fenian leader Jeremiah O'Donovan Rossa. Pearse followed Clarke's instructions to make his speech 'as hot as hell' and delivered a rousing address, culminating with the lines:

> But the fools, the fools, the fools! – they have left us our Fenian dead, and while Ireland holds these graves, Ireland unfree shall never be at peace.

The speech was widely reported in the newspapers and Pearse became well known outside nationalist circles. A month later he became a member of the Supreme Council of the IRB and from this point was part of the inner circle that would decide when a rebellion would take place. Pearse began to write up his political ideas and his thoughts on the rationale for a rebellion. He completed four pamphlets in December 1915, and they were published in the early months of 1916. The pamphlets

– *Ghosts, The Separatist Ideal, The Sovereign People* and *The Spiritual Nation* – focused on Pearse's interpretation of the political philosophy of four men whom he considered to be the fathers of Irish republicanism: Wolfe Tone, John Mitchel, Thomas Davis and James Fintan Lalor.

In the week before the Easter Rising, Pearse was central to preparations for the rebellion and was also a key player in the events that threatened to tear plans for rebellion asunder. Pearse and other radical members of the IRB had kept details of the rebellion from Eoin MacNeill, the commander-in-chief of the Irish Volunteers. MacNeill and some of the more moderate members of the IRB, such as Bulmer Hobson and Michael O'Rahilly, saw a rebellion as justified only if the government tried to suppress the Irish Volunteers or introduce conscription. During Holy Week, MacNeill came to suspect that a rebellion was being planned and in the early hours of Good Friday he went to St Enda's to confront Pearse, who confirmed that a rising would take place and told MacNeill there was little he could do to stop it. MacNeill and Pearse had been friends since Pearse's earliest days in the Gaelic League and MacNeill felt betrayed.

Later that morning Pearse, Seán Mac Diarmada and Thomas MacDonagh went to MacNeill's home to inform him of plans that day to land German arms in Co. Kerry. At this point, MacNeill seems to have been resigned to the fact that some sort of insurrection was inevitable. On Holy Saturday news came through that the boat carrying the arms had been scuttled and that Roger Casement, who had been in Germany to arrange for German support for the rebellion and had landed at Banna Strand, Co. Kerry, from a German U-boat, had been arrested. This prompted MacNeill to issue a countermanding order to the Volunteers, instructing them not to mobilise on Easter Sunday as planned. A notice of this countermanding order was placed in the *Sunday Independent*.

Pearse attended a meeting of the Supreme Council of the IRB at Liberty Hall on Easter Sunday, at which it was decided to postpone the Rising until the following day. A draft Proclamation of the Irish Republic, mostly written by Pearse, had already been ratified by the seven-member Supreme Council, who now made up the provisional government of the Irish Republic. The document was finalised at this meeting and Pearse was appointed to the posts of president of the provisional government of the Irish Republic and commandant-general of the army of the Irish Republic. The following morning, Pearse spent a couple of hours arranging his affairs at the Hermitage. He and Willie then said goodbye to their mother and sisters, before leaving St Enda's for the last time.

At 11.50 a.m. on Easter Monday the Volunteers assembled at Liberty Hall to begin their march to the GPO. Shortly before, Pearse's sister Mary Brighid had arrived to plead with Patrick to abandon his plans and return home, but as James Connolly, commandant of the forces in Dublin, marched at the head of the column, Pearse was just behind him. The Volunteers evacuated the GPO of its customers and staff, arrested some policemen and soldiers present and began to fortify the building. At 12.45 p.m. Pearse stepped out onto the street and read aloud the Proclamation to a small and confused crowd gathered there. Returning inside the GPO, Desmond FitzGerald observed that Pearse looked 'deeply moved' as he surveyed the men who had turned out for the rebellion. Just hours later, though, his look of pride was replaced by one of dismay as he watched the people of Dublin looting the shops on Sackville Street.[10]

Although Pearse held the position of commander-in-chief, he was not a natural military leader and throughout Easter Week it was Connolly who gave orders to the rebels. Pearse took charge of propaganda, writing the bulletin *Irish War News* and issuing manifestos to the people of Dublin. From Wednesday the GPO came under heavy attack from a combination of sniper fire, machine-gun fire, field artillery bombardment and shelling. By Thursday the rebels were struggling to resist the onslaught by British forces. Pearse addressed the garrison, telling them that Volunteers were arriving from Dundalk and Wexford, giving them false hope that help was on the way.

Pearse was a source of inspiration for the Volunteers, both in his words and his actions, right up to their surrender. In his manifesto issued on Thursday, Pearse praised his forces and assured them of the righteousness of their actions:

I desire now, lest I may not have an opportunity later, to pay homage to the gallantry of the Soldiers of Irish Freedom who have during the past four days been writing with fire and steel the most glorious chapter in the later history of Ireland. Justice can never be done to their heroism, to their discipline, to their gay and unconquerable spirit, in the midst of peril and death. ... If they do not win this fight, they will at least have deserved to win it. But win it they will, although they may win it in death. Already they have won a great thing. They have redeemed Dublin from many shames, and made her name splendid among the names of Cities.[11]

At 8.00 p.m. on Friday the rebels could no longer hold the GPO and the order to evacuate was given. After the Volunteers had left, Frank Henderson recalled, Pearse risked his personal safety to 'take a final look round the G.P.O. to make absolutely certain that nobody had been left behind'.[12]

The rebels retreated to houses on Moore Street, which became their headquarters. At noon on Saturday the leaders held a meeting to plan their next move. Pearse is believed to have been influenced in his decision to surrender by an incident that occurred on Moore Street. Three elderly men were lying on the street, having been shot dead as they left their homes. This convinced Pearse of the need to end the fighting and later, in the order for surrender, he wrote of his desire 'to prevent the further slaughter of Dublin citizens'.[13] Although Clarke, the most senior member of the provisional government, resisted the surrender, the other leaders present decided to lay down arms.

At around 12.45 p.m. Pearse instructed Elizabeth O'Farrell, a member of the ICA, to approach the military cordon carrying a white flag and to inform the officers there that the Volunteers wished to discuss surrender terms. However, the commanding officer, Brigadier General W. H. M. Lowe, insisted on an unconditional surrender. At 3.30 p.m., accompanied by O'Farrell, Pearse walked to the top of Moore Street and surrendered to Lowe. He was brought to Parkgate Barracks, where he met with the British commander-in-chief, General Sir John Maxwell. From the barracks he issued an order that all rebel outposts were to surrender.

Pearse was held in Arbour Hill Prison from Saturday 29 April, separating him from the majority of the other leaders, who were held at Richmond Barracks. On Tuesday 2 May he was transferred to Richmond Barracks to face his court martial, which was presided over by Brigadier General C. G. Blackader. Three prosecution witnesses were called and Pearse chose not to cross-examine any of them. A letter he had written to his mother from Arbour Hill, describing the final hours of the rebels in the GPO and their surrender, was produced as evidence against him. Pearse made a statement to the court martial in which he outlined his reason for surrendering and he expressed the hope that his 'followers' would receive an amnesty:

I went down on my knees as a child and told God that I would work all my life to gain the freedom of Ireland. I have deemed it my duty as an Irishman to fight for the freedom of my country. I admit I have organised men to fight against Britain. I admit having opened negotiations with Germany. We have kept our word with her and as far as I can see she did her best to help us. She sent a ship with arms. Germany has not sent us gold.[14]

He was sentenced to death by firing squad and shortly afterwards the sentence was approved by Maxwell. Pearse was transferred to Kilmainham Gaol to await his execution the following morning.

In his final days he composed four poems. Three were written at Arbour Hill – 'To My Mother', 'To My Brother' and 'A Mother Speaks' – while his final poem, 'The Wayfarer', was written in Kilmainham Gaol. In the poem 'To My Brother' he reflected on the close relationship he had shared with Willie:

> O faithful!
> Moulded in one womb,
> We two have stood together all the years,
> All the glad years and all the sorrowful years,
> Own brothers: through good repute and ill

Right up until his death, Pearse assumed that his brother Willie would avoid execution as he had not held a position of leadership in the Rising. He died not knowing that Willie would also face the firing squad on 4 May. According to Fr Aloysius, the Capuchin priest who attended Pearse before his execution, an attempt was made to bring Margaret Pearse Snr to see her son at Kilmainham Gaol. Fr Aloysius was present in a military car that he later discovered was travelling to collect Mrs Pearse at the Hermitage in Rathfarnham. However, the car was held up by sniper fire at Charlemont Bridge in the city centre and was forced to head directly to Kilmainham without her.[15] Pearse spent his final hours writing letters to his mother and his brother and was given the last rites by Fr Aloysius. Patrick Pearse was the first of the leaders of the Easter Rising to be executed, at 3.30 a.m. on 3 May 1916.

THOMAS CLARKE

Thomas Clarke, the oldest of the executed leaders of the Easter Rising, was born at an unlikely location: the British Army barracks at Hurst Castle, Isle of Wight, on 11 March 1858. His father, Thomas Snr, was an officer in the British Army and had served during the Crimean War. He was a native of Co. Leitrim and his wife, Mary (née Palmer), was from Co. Tipperary. Thomas Snr was subsequently transferred to South Africa and the Clarkes spent some years living in various British Army garrison towns in that country. In 1865 Clarke's father attained the rank of battery sergeant and the family transferred to Dungannon, Co. Tyrone.[1] For Thomas, who moved around so much as a young child, Dungannon was the closest to a home place he ever had. According to his friend and associate Seán McGarry: 'Tom always retained a great love for Dungannon of which he regarded himself as a native.'[2]

Clarke attended national school in the town and was later appointed monitor, the role given to older pupils who worked as classroom assistants. According to McGarry, Clarke may well have become a teacher except that he refused to work on a Sunday, when he was required to teach catechism to the younger pupils at the school. Clarke objected to working outside normal teaching hours.

It was in Dungannon that Clarke first engaged with radical nationalist politics. In 1878 John Daly, the IRB organiser who later played a prominent role in Clarke's life, visited the town. Clarke was greatly taken with what Daly had to say and the well-known Fenian swore him into the IRB. William Kelly, a fellow classmate of Clarke's at the national school in Dungannon, was initiated into the IRB two years after him, in 1880. At this point Kelly noted that Clarke was at the centre of the IRB circle in Dungannon, which consisted of twenty-three members. John Daly returned to the town shortly afterwards and advised the IRB to begin training and drilling in preparation for 'taking military action against the RIC'.[3]

On 15 August 1880 a riot broke out between members of the Orange Order and members of the Ancient Order of Hibernians, who were parading for the Catholic feast of the Assumption. The RIC intervened and opened fire on the riot; one man was shot dead. The following night Clarke, Kelly and up to four other members of the IRB ambushed a group of RIC men on Irish Street but were forced to retreat when reinforcements arrived. Fearing repercussions for his involvement in the ambush, Clarke decided to emigrate to America. Before leaving he made contact with Camp No. 1 of Clan na Gael, the Irish-American revolutionary organisation which had formal links with the IRB in Ireland. On arrival in New York Clarke was welcomed by Clan member Patrick O'Connor, who provided him with employment in his shoe shop. In the spring of 1881 Clarke found other work as a night porter at the Mansion House Hotel, Brooklyn.

During this period Clan na Gael were involved in organising a bombing campaign in England. In America they trained men in the use of chemicals and arranged for their passage to England, where they were to participate in a plan to detonate explosives. Clarke's growing involvement with the Clan in America coincided with this development, and in the summer of 1881 he was part of a group of 'prospective dynamitards' who were shown how to make and use explosives by Dr Thomas Gallagher.[4]

In early 1883 Clarke was preparing to take up a management position at a hotel in Brighton Beach when he was ordered by Clan na Gael to prepare for a secret voyage to England. He set sail shortly afterwards, travelling under the alias Henry Hammond Wilson. On arrival in England, he lodged in the Southwark area of London. Unknown to Clarke and his co-conspirators, including Dr Gallagher and James Murphy (known by his alias, Alfred Whitehead), they had aroused the suspicion of police officers who were now trailing them. Clarke was arrested at his lodgings on 5 April 1883. Whitehead had been arrested in Birmingham the day before, and Clarke and Gallagher were reading about the arrest in a newspaper when the police swooped to take them into custody. Clarke was tried in the Old Bailey, where prosecution witnesses included a cab driver and a train station worker who had observed him carrying a large and heavy portmanteau. He was using this case to transport liquid explosives, which were discovered during his arrest.

On 14 June 1883 Clarke, along with three other Fenians, was found guilty of treason felony and sentenced to life imprisonment. He was first held at Millbank Prison, before being transferred to Chatham Prison in December 1883. Clarke suffered the worst of the Victorian prison regime, with treason-felony prisoners subjected to particularly harsh conditions. He later wrote about his experience in the memoir *Glimpses of an Irish Felon's Prison Life*, which recounted the relentless monotony of the system of silence and separation:

Had anyone told me before the prison doors closed upon me that it was possible for any human being to endure what the Irish prisoners have endured in Chatham Prison, and come out of it alive and sane, I would not have believed him, yet some have done so, and it has been a source of perpetual surprise to me that I was able to get through it all.[5]

As a treason-felony prisoner, Clarke and the other Fenians were not held in the main hall of the prison along with the other convict prisoners but were kept separate in small penal cells. According to Clarke, their separation from the main body of prisoners allowed the guards to engage in 'a scientific system of perpetual and persistent harassing'.[6] This included sleep deprivation, where the guards would deliberately slam shut a heavy iron trapdoor when carrying out checks on the prisoners at night-time, to wake them. During his imprisonment Clarke worked as a moulder in the iron foundry and this laborious work was made more difficult by the fact that he was often on bread and water punishment while working on heavy castings.

In 1884 Clarke's imprisonment was made somewhat more bearable by the arrival to Chatham of John Daly, his mentor from his days with the IRB in Dungannon. Like Clarke, Daly had been arrested for possession of explosives, at Wolverhampton train station. Although the operation of the silent system at Chatham meant that Clarke could not speak to Daly, his presence in the prison along with his IRB colleague James

Francis Egan gave him 'support and encouragement'. Clarke devised a type of Morse code system of knocking on the walls of the cells to allow for some communication between the Fenian convicts.

But the bar on communication, as well as the harshness of the regime, took its toll. Gallagher and Whitehead suffered a total breakdown of their mental health while at Chatham. Clarke was admitted to the prison hospital several times during his fifteen years of imprisonment. Meanwhile at home in Ireland an Amnesty Association was formed to campaign for the release of the Fenian prisoners. Clarke's case was championed by the socialite and political activist Maud Gonne, and after 1896 by John Daly, who was released from prison on medical grounds. Clarke was finally released from prison on 29 September 1898 and he came to Dublin, where his mother and sister were now living in Kilmainham.

As part of the reception held to welcome him home to Ireland, Clarke was awarded the freedom of Limerick city on 2 March 1899. It was during his visit to Limerick that he met Kathleen Daly, John Daly's niece. She was unimpressed by him when they first met:

> I was keenly disappointed. His appearance gave no indication of the kingly, heroic qualities which Uncle John had told us about; there was none of the conquering hero which I had visioned. He was emaciated and stooped from the long imprisonment and hardship.[7]

In spite of this poor first impression, they began exchanging letters, and continued to correspond with each other when Clarke emigrated to America with his sister Maria in 1899. He found work there as a pattern maker in the Cameron Pump Works in New York and in his letters he encouraged Kathleen to join him in America so that they could be married. The match met with the disapproval of the Daly family, not least because of the significant age gap of twenty-one years. But Kathleen was determined to marry Tom and she travelled to New York, where they were married on 16 July 1901. John MacBride, the Fenian veteran of the Boer War, was their best man.

Kathleen and Tom set up home at Greenpoint, Brooklyn, and their first son, Daly, was born in 1902. Clarke lost his job at Cameron Pump Works and the young couple set up an ice-cream and sweet shop. Clarke resumed his activities with Clan na Gael, encouraging John Devoy, the leading member of the organisation, to establish a newspaper. Clarke subsequently became manager of the *Gaelic American*, with Devoy as its editor. Throughout this period of the early twentieth century, the relationship between America and Great Britain grew closer and an Anglo-American alliance was proposed. Clarke was involved with Irish-American organisations which tried to thwart this alliance by highlighting the cause of Irish independence.

Kathleen found life in New York difficult. It was hard for her to adjust to apartment living in Brooklyn, where she had to learn to make no noise so as not to disturb her neighbours. She and her son suffered bad health and had to return to Ireland for a few months in 1905 for Daly to recover from a bout of diphtheria. Kathleen was advised by her doctor to move to the countryside for the sake of her health, and her uncle, John Daly, bought a farm for the Clarkes on Long Island. Because of its distance from New York, Clarke had to resign his post with the *Gaelic American*.

Although the family were fairly content with their life on Long Island, Clarke began to itch to go home. One of his greatest disappointments was that there had been no rebellion in Ireland at the turn of the twentieth century, when the British Army was preoccupied with fighting in the Boer War. Growing tensions between Britain and Germany suggested the possibility of a war between these two countries. Clarke was motivated to return to Ireland to plan for a rebellion at a time when England's attention would be diverted by another foreign war. Clarke was also impressed with Bulmer Hobson, an IRB member who toured America in 1907. Buoyed by the prospect of a new generation reinvigorating the Fenian movement, Clarke decided to return to Ireland with his family.

Kathleen's sister Madge assisted the Clarkes with the purchase of a newsagents in Dublin in January 1908. Their first shop was located at 77 Amiens Street, and in 1909 they purchased another shop at 75a Parnell Street. Clarke threw himself into IRB activities and was co-opted onto the organisation's Supreme Council. He became president of the North Dock Ward Branch of Sinn Féin and organised commemorations of Wolfe Tone at his grave in Bodenstown. Clarke tried to rejuvenate the IRB by focusing his attention on the younger generation and he formed a close relationship with Seán Mac Diarmada, an up-and-coming political activist. In 1910 he was involved in the establishment of the *Irish Freedom* newspaper, which was to be a mouthpiece for the IRB. Clarke was chair of the editorial committee and its other members were drawn from the more youthful side of the organisation: Hobson, Mac Diarmada, Pat McCartan, Piaras Béaslaí and Seán McGarry. Clarke also facilitated the entry of Patrick Pearse into the IRB, by giving him the opportunity to speak at a commemoration for Robert Emmet in 1911 and by publishing his articles in *Irish Freedom*.

In 1911 Clarke succeeded in ousting the older generation of the IRB, including Fred Allan, chair of the Supreme Council. Clarke, along with Mac Diarmada and Hobson, was now in control of the IRB, and his shop on Parnell Street became the hub of the organisation. McGarry later recalled that 'from this time forward Tom became the pivot of the whole separatist movement'.[8]

Another turning point came with the formation of the Irish Volunteers in November 1913. Clarke saw the potential in this organisation to provide a revolutionary force for the rebellion he anticipated would take place if Britain went to war. Although he supported the formation of the Irish Volunteers, Clarke did not become a member of its Provisional Committee. He preferred to remain in the background to avoid bringing himself to the attention of the authorities. In June 1914 the leader of the Irish Parliamentary Party, John Redmond, sought to exert control over the growing membership of the Irish Volunteers by seeking to nominate twenty-five members of the Provisional Committee. Bulmer Hobson was alone among the IRB men on the committee who supported Redmond's proposal. Clarke was disgusted by his actions and never spoke again to Hobson, who subsequently resigned from the Supreme Council of the IRB.

Clarke and Mac Diarmada were not directly involved in the landing of arms at Howth on 26 July 1914 until they received word that soldiers were seen boarding a tram headed for the seaside village that afternoon. They immediately took a cab to Howth, where they met some Volunteers and filled their cab with arms, making as many return journeys as they could to bring the rifles back to Dublin. Clarke later ensured that some of these rifles were distributed to the Irish Volunteer corps in his native Dungannon.

Following Redmond's speech at Woodenbridge in September 1914, the Irish Volunteers split between those who supported Irishmen being part of the British war effort and those who opposed Irishmen joining the British Army. Clarke and Mac Diarmada were overjoyed at this division, which meant that Redmond could no longer exert his influence over the remaining Irish Volunteers, leaving them free to set the organisation on the path to rebellion.[9] At a meeting chaired by Clarke at the library of the Gaelic League on 9 September

1914 it was decided that the war in Europe would be used as an opportunity to stage a rebellion in Ireland.

Throughout 1915 Clarke played a central role in orchestrating plans for the rebellion, although he continued to do so as a background figure. The government had in December 1914 suppressed *Irish Freedom* and Clarke and Mac Diarmada were behind the establishment of the replacement newspaper, *Nationality*, in 1915, of which Mac Diarmada was manager. The arrest and imprisonment of Mac Diarmada from May to September 1915 came as a blow to Clarke, both personally and from an organisational point of view.

Clarke opposed Roger Casement's efforts to travel to Germany via the USA to seek arms and support for a rebellion in Ireland. He instructed John Devoy in America to have nothing to do with him. As with Hobson, a rift had developed between Clarke and Casement over the latter's support for Redmond in the controversy over the twenty-five nominees. Clarke's concerns were heightened when Casement reached Germany, as he believed that Casement did not have full knowledge of 'the actual situation in Ireland'.[10] Clarke sent Robert Monteith to follow Casement to Germany to keep an eye on him.

A military committee of the IRB, including Patrick Pearse, Joseph Plunkett and Éamonn Ceannt, had been formed to plan the rebellion. Clarke and Mac Diarmada joined the committee in September 1915, and this became the new Supreme Council of the IRB. They held the positions of secretary and treasurer, and had Denis McCullough, an IRB man living in

Belfast, elected as chair. McCullough's distance from Dublin ensured that Clarke and Mac Diarmada 'effectively controlled the supreme council'.[11]

Clarke's greatest triumph in 1915 was undoubtedly his role as director of arrangements for the funeral of Jeremiah O'Donovan Rossa. He chaired the committee set up on 1 August and was given free rein by Devoy to plan the funeral as he saw fit. According to McGarry, the O'Donovan Rossa funeral allowed Clarke to demonstrate 'his great capacity for work, his power of organisation and his complete mastery of details'.[12] Clarke succeeded in bringing together many nationalist organisations for the funeral and his decision to ask Pearse to deliver the graveside oration showed his foresight in realising the potential of Pearse's powerful oratory. Large crowds attended the funeral and it was a rallying point for nationalists ahead of the rebellion in 1916.

By Easter Week 1916 Clarke looked much older than his fifty-nine years. His fifteen years of imprisonment had taken its toll and he was a small, thin, greying man. Nonetheless he was respected among republicans as a figurehead for the movement. On Tuesday evening of Holy Week he returned to his home in Ballybough to tell Kathleen that a rising would take place the following Sunday. He also informed her that he had been proposed as the first signatory of the Proclamation of the Irish Republic and that Thomas MacDonagh had refused to sign the document until Clarke had done so, believing that 'no other man was entitled to the honour'.[13]

But the plans that Clarke had so carefully masterminded began to fall apart on Good Friday. The arrest of Roger Casement in Co. Kerry and the scuttling of the *Aud* with its cargo of arms prompted Eoin MacNeill to issue a countermanding order calling off the Rising late on Holy Saturday. At a meeting of the Supreme Council at Liberty Hall on Easter Sunday, Clarke was the only council member to argue for a rebellion to go ahead that evening. He was eventually persuaded to delay until the following day. McGarry recalled a conversation with Clarke that evening, when Clarke was still contemplating the impact of the order:

> The shock of the morning's blow had been terrific. I accompanied him home that evening. He was very silent. After a while he recovered and discussed the affair. He regarded McNeill's [*sic*] action was of the blackest and greatest treachery. But having said all he wanted to say about it he did not refer to it again.[14]

He spent the night of Easter Sunday at home, with McGarry and another IRB man acting as bodyguards.

Clarke was too frail to march to the GPO with the Irish Volunteers on the morning of 24 April 1916. He travelled by car and on arrival he helped the Volunteers to smash the windows of the building. He stood by Pearse outside the GPO while the latter read aloud the Proclamation. Throughout Easter Week he did not wear a uniform, nor did he hold a military position in the new army of an Irish Republic.

Nonetheless he was acknowledged by the garrison at the GPO as a person whose orders should be obeyed. McGarry observed that Clarke remained calm and collected during the week in the GPO, giving orders 'decisively and as calmly as if he were in his own shop'.[15] On Tuesday evening Clarke explained his reasoning behind organising the rebellion to Min Ryan, a Cumann na mBan courier from Wexford:

> The gist of it was – that people naturally would now be against them for rising and coming out like this; that one of the reasons for people being against them would be because of the counter-manding order, but that they had come to this conclusion that it was absolutely necessary that they should have this Rising now, because if they did not have it now, they might never have it ...[16]

It is clear that from the time of his return from America in 1907, Clarke was determined not to repeat the mistake of the past by failing to have a rebellion during a time of war.

Kathleen remained at home during Easter Week and received updates from the GPO from messengers. Her brother, Ned Daly, was also in action during the rebellion, commanding at the Four Courts. By Friday Kathleen no longer needed the couriers to keep her informed of developments as she became keenly aware of events by watching from her bedroom window:

> That night I watched, from the upper windows of the house, the smoke and flames of what seemed to be the whole city in flames.

I watched all night; it seemed to me no one could escape from that inferno. The picture of my husband and brother caught in it was vividly before me, and their helplessness against that raging fire appalled me.[17]

The fires witnessed by Kathleen forced the inevitable evacuation of the GPO. Clarke was with the other leaders who retreated to Moore Street and convened a military council to discuss their options. Again he proved to be the most determined of the revolutionaries, objecting to the surrender proposed by Pearse and arguing that the rebels should fight on. He broke down in tears when the decision was taken to seek terms.

Following the surrender, the Volunteers spent Saturday night sleeping in the open in the gardens of the Rotunda Hospital. Witnesses described seeing Clarke being very roughly handled by British officers, including Captain Lea Wilson. Michael Collins witnessed this treatment and subsequently ordered the assassination of Wilson during the War of Independence.

Along with the rest of the GPO garrison, Clarke was marched from the Rotunda to Richmond Barracks in Inchicore on Sunday morning. Liam Ó Briain, a fellow prisoner, recalled seeing Clarke sleeping side by side with Seán Mac Diarmada that night, Mac Diarmada's head lying on Clarke's lap.[18] Clarke was court-martialled on 2 May 1916. As he had done at his trial for treason felony almost thirty-three years previously, Clarke cross-examined the sole witness produced by the prosecution. Lieutenant S. L. King of the Royal Inniskilling

Fusiliers testified that he was held prisoner in the GPO during the Rising and that he considered that Clarke held a position of authority among the rebels. Clarke did not call any witnesses in his defence, nor did he make a statement to the court. He was found guilty and was sentenced to death by firing squad.

Kathleen Clarke was arrested at her home in Ballybough on the same morning as her husband's court martial, 2 May. She was held for the day in Dublin Castle and that evening she was brought to Kilmainham Gaol, where her husband was to be shot at dawn the following morning. On entering his cell the first thing she asked him was why the rebels had surrendered. He replied that he had been outvoted by the other leaders on the matter. He told her that he had dismissed the priest who had been attending him, as the priest wanted him to express sorrow for his part in the rebellion before he would give him absolution. Tom told Kathleen:

> I told him to clear out of my cell quickly. I was not sorry for what I had done, I gloried in it and the men who had been with me. To say I was sorry would be a lie, and I was not going to face my God with a lie on my tongue.[19]

Kathleen was pregnant at the time of Tom's execution but she did not tell him that she was carrying their child during her last visit with him. According to Kathleen he was in 'an exalted frame of mind' when she left him. Tom Clarke was executed at dawn on 3 May 1916.

Thomas MacDonagh

Thomas MacDonagh, poet, teacher, literary critic and signatory of the 1916 Proclamation, was born at Cloughjordan, Co. Tipperary, on 1 February 1878. Like some of the other leaders of the Easter Rising, MacDonagh's Irish identity was a complex one. His mother, Mary (née Parker), was the daughter of English parents. She met and married Joseph MacDonagh while they were both working as national schoolteachers in

Cloghan, Co. Offaly. Thomas was the eldest surviving child of the MacDonagh family; three siblings born before him died in infancy. He had two sisters and three brothers. His mother seems to have been the strongest influence on the young Thomas. She converted to Catholicism shortly before her marriage and was a very pious woman. Mary was also a writer and MacDonagh grew up reading her poems, short stories and religious writings.

At the age of fourteen MacDonagh began attending Rockwell College near Cashel, Co. Tipperary, a private school run by the Holy Ghost Fathers. This religious order had its origins in France and it was at Rockwell that MacDonagh learned to speak French fluently, a language that he would later teach. In 1894 MacDonagh decided to begin his studies to become a Holy Ghost Father, writing to the superior to request 'the holy habit of the Congregation that I may become in a manner a sharer of all privileges which are conferred on the Scholastics of the holy Congregation'.[1] However, in 1901 MacDonagh found that he no longer had a vocation for the priesthood and withdrew from his studies. He continued to teach at the school, and in 1902 his first collection of poetry, *Through the Ivory Gate*, was published. He dedicated the volume to the poet W. B. Yeats, from whom he had sought advice on his poetry writing. The dedication indicated MacDonagh's intention to become a writer who would be taken seriously in Irish literary circles.

MacDonagh left Rockwell in 1901 to teach English,

history and French at St Kieran's College, Kilkenny. It was the first Catholic college to open in Ireland after the penal laws, which restricted the education of Catholics, were relaxed. While working in Kilkenny, MacDonagh attended his first meeting of the Gaelic League. Apparently he attended the meeting with a friend with the intention of poking fun at the Irish speakers, but he was very taken by the enthusiasm of the Gaelic League members for the revival of the Irish language and became a dedicated member. 'His conversion to the Irish Ireland creed had been as startling as the conversion of St Paul,' wrote his former pupil Desmond Ryan.[2] With the zeal of a convert he threw himself into organising work for the Kilkenny branch of Gaelic League, carrying out fund-raising and co-ordinating Irish Language Week in the town in March 1903.

In June of the same year he left St Kieran's and Kilkenny. His biographer, Johann Norstedt, has suggested that his position 'became untenable because of his new preoccupation'.[3] MacDonagh left his post in St Kieran's without having obtained another teaching position, an unusual move for someone in straitened financial circumstances. It may have been the case that management at St Kieran's was not as supportive of an Irish ethos as MacDonagh would have liked. This is borne out by his comment in a letter to his friend Dominic Hackett that his new school, St Colman's in Fermoy, Co. Cork, was 'a very different place from St K's. Gaelic to the spine.'[4]

From 1903 to 1908 MacDonagh taught at St Colman's

and attended meetings of the local branch of the Gaelic League. He also devoted himself to his writing during this period, publishing a poetry collection, *The Golden Joy*, in 1907. He worked in earnest on his first play, *When the Dawn is Come*, revising his drafts several times on the advice of Yeats and J. M. Synge. The play, centred around the character of a poet, Thurlough, and set in Ireland fifty years in the future, was eventually staged at the Abbey Theatre in October 1908. *When the Dawn is Come* foreshadowed MacDonagh's own involvement in revolution some years later, as Thurlough finds himself leading an Irish army in a rebellion against foreign rulers. It received a lukewarm reception from the critics, although the audiences were enthused. MacDonagh criticised the poor production of the play by the Abbey Theatre.

The opening of a bilingual school for boys by Patrick Pearse in Dublin provided MacDonagh with the opportunity to move closer to the literary and nationalist circles he longed to be a part of. His appointment as second master at St Enda's in September 1908 reflected his teaching experience and his prominence in the Gaelic League. St Enda's espoused the Irish Ireland values that MacDonagh now so earnestly supported, and the innovative teaching methods proposed by Pearse excited him. MacDonagh used the Direct Method to teach Irish and French, conducting his classes through the medium of the target language. He frequently promised his pupils that they could make dramatic progress quickly, telling them that if they worked hard they could become fluent Irish speakers within six months. But as a teacher MacDonagh was easily distracted and one past pupil, Desmond Ryan, remembered how students would ask 'artful leading questions' to set him off talking on another topic.[5] Milo McGarry, also a St Enda's boy, recalled how MacDonagh began a system in the school where one teacher would sit at each of the boys' tables in the refectory. Mealtimes became another lesson for McGarry, when MacDonagh would share his knowledge of a wide range of topics. But what impressed him most was how MacDonagh spoke to him 'as an adult'.[6]

Descriptions of MacDonagh, both as a teacher at St Enda's and elsewhere, refer to him as a small, lively, talkative man, always joking with the people he encountered. A fellow student of MacDonagh's at Rockwell College remembered how MacDonagh 'gave the impression that he wore a smile constantly and a slight prominence in his teeth heightened that impression'.[7] Desmond Ryan observed that he could become friendly with a classroom of forty boys within ten minutes.

Yet although he seemed at ease in the company of others, MacDonagh often preferred his own company. From 1910 he lived on the rural outskirts of Dublin city in Rathfarnham, renting the gate lodge of a house belonging to David Houston. It was there, according to his friend and fellow writer James Stephens, that MacDonagh lived a 'semi-detached life', balancing both his 'longing for a hermit's existence' and his 'gift for gregarious life'.[8]

Living in Dublin allowed MacDonagh to meet with fellow

writers and provided new opportunities for his development as a poet and playwright. Stephens, Padraic Colum and George Russell visited him at the gate lodge. But his most regular visitor was Joseph Plunkett, whom MacDonagh met when he responded to an advertisement seeking an Irish teacher for private lessons. Their friendship developed rapidly, based on a shared interest in writing poetry and a desire to critique each other's work. Plunkett's sister Geraldine thought that the pair more or less 'haunted each other', frequenting each other's homes nearly every day.[9] Another important meeting for MacDonagh around this time occurred when he met his future wife, Muriel Gifford, who accompanied the suffragette Nannie Dryhurst when she came to St Enda's to speak with the boys.

In 1910 MacDonagh graduated from University College Dublin (UCD) with a Bachelor of Arts degree, having read English, French and Irish while also teaching at St Enda's. He left the school in 1910 for reasons that are uncertain. He may have been unhappy about the school moving to Rathfarnham, but he was also contemplating moving to Paris, where he spent six weeks during the summer of 1910. MacDonagh and Pearse parted on cordial terms and he wrote to Gertrude Bloomer, the headmistress at the sister school for girls, St Ita's, telling her that he still believed St Enda's was 'the best school for boys in Ireland'.[10]

By January 1911 he was back teaching part-time at St Enda's while working on his MA thesis on the life of the

Elizabethan poet Thomas Campion. In March MacDonagh's growing circle of literary friends led to his involvement in *The Irish Review*, a monthly arts journal which he co-founded with Colum, Stephens and Mary Maguire. His friend and landlord in Rathfarnham, David Houston, provided financial backing. The journal provided an outlet for the publication of MacDonagh's writings, including a play, *Metempsychosis.*

The year 1911 also saw the development of his relationship with Muriel Gifford, although MacDonagh had been recently bruised by a love affair with Mary Maguire, a teacher at St Ita's who later married their mutual friend, Padraic Colum. MacDonagh and Gifford's relationship was kept secret from her parents for some time. Muriel was the daughter of a Catholic father and Protestant mother and had been raised in the Protestant faith. Her relationship with MacDonagh, a Catholic, would have been met with some disapproval. They were married on 8 January 1912, with Pearse chosen as his best man. But when Pearse failed to arrive on time for the ceremony, a man who was clipping the hedges outside instead stood in as witness.

This was a happy period in MacDonagh's life. He was working as a lecturer in UCD and his first child, Donagh, was born in November 1912. His involvement in *The Irish Review* increased when MacDonagh arranged for Plunkett to buy out the journal when it ran into financial difficulties in 1913. With Plunkett as editor, MacDonagh contributed more articles to the magazine and was heavily involved in its production.

Before 1913 there is no evidence of MacDonagh's involvement in nationalist politics. However, from November 1913 onwards *The Irish Review* became less a literary journal and more a political one. Plunkett and MacDonagh published several articles relating to the Irish Volunteers, including the organisation's manifesto and a 'Marching Song' composed by MacDonagh, to be sung by the Volunteers while on drill practice:

For Ireland, for Ireland, for Ireland all,
Our ranks we band in might:
From her four seas we at Ireland's call
In Ireland's cause unite,
And march to the hosting of Gael and Gall,
To claim our freedom's right.[11]

MacDonagh's decision to join the Irish Volunteers in December 1913 may have been influenced by the fact that his friends – including Pearse and his colleague Eoin MacNeill at UCD – were prominent in the movement. In spite of his lack of experience, MacDonagh's advancement in the Irish Volunteers was rapid. He spoke at recruitment meetings for the organisation around Ireland and in July 1914 he was appointed commandant of the 2nd Battalion, Dublin Brigade. MacDonagh was involved in the Howth gun-running later that month. During the subsequent split in the Irish Volunteers, MacDonagh sided with the minority who opposed John Redmond. In the new, significantly smaller Volunteers, he was appointed director of training in the organisation.

The articles included in *The Irish Review* became more radical as the political climate intensified, culminating in MacDonagh's article 'Twenty Plain Facts for the Irishman' published in the final edition of *The Irish Review* in late 1914. MacDonagh declared that 'the Irishman who says he would prefer to be under English rule than under German rule is a slave'.[12]

MacDonagh continued with his literary activities. His thesis on Thomas Campion had been published in 1913, as had a volume of poetry entitled *Lyrical Poems*. He was also involved in the establishment of the Irish Theatre on Hardwicke Street with Plunkett and Edward Martyn, and his one-act play, *Pagans*, was performed at the Irish Theatre in April 1915. But it was clear that the focus and energy of MacDonagh's life had shifted from literature to politics and in a letter to his friend Dominic Hackett, written shortly after the birth of his daughter, Barbara, MacDonagh wrote:

> I have found a great thing to do in and with life outside the very real and wonderful interest that a wife and two children give me. It is worth living in Ireland as one of the directors of the Irish Volunteers. We have done more for our generation, thank God, than any of the men of the other periods did since the old clan times, more than the '98 men or Emmet or the '48 or '67 men. We are making preparations. Destiny will take charge of the issue.[13]

In July 1915 MacDonagh's prominence in nationalist politics was confirmed when he was appointed to the funeral committee directed by Thomas Clarke that organised the funeral of the Fenian leader Jeremiah O'Donovan Rossa.

Compared with the other signatories of the Proclamation, MacDonagh was not privy to the plans for a rebellion until late on in their development. He did not become aware of the details until he was co-opted onto the Supreme Council of the IRB in early April 1916, shortly before the Rising was due to take place. His brother John recalled that Thomas informed him of the rebellion three weeks before it was due to take place. As Easter approached, MacDonagh began to give strong indications to his battalion of Volunteers that a rising was imminent. Seamus Daly, a member of the 2nd Battalion, recalled a meeting of his Volunteer company on Holy Thursday at Father Mathew Park in Fairview, Dublin, where MacDonagh addressed the men for longer than usual:

> He … reminded us that we were standing on historic ground in Clontarf where Brian Boru had defeated the Danes in 1014. Easter was the time of the battle of Clontarf. The battle was on Good Friday. Good Friday and Easter were coming near, and that was the time of resurgence in Ireland, and who knows but it might be resurgence in Ireland, and he was glad to see we were all ready to take part in it …[14]

During the week before the Easter Rising, MacDonagh's main

involvement in preparations for the rebellion was to negotiate with Eoin MacNeill on behalf of the Supreme Council of the IRB. As a close colleague of MacNeill's he was an obvious choice for this role, and on Good Friday morning he went with Seán Mac Diarmada to MacNeill's home to inform him of the imminent landing of arms from Germany in Co. Kerry. According to his brother John, he also met with MacNeill on Holy Saturday evening and on Sunday morning, emerging from the Saturday meeting 'rather agitated', knowing that MacNeill's countermanding order had scuppered plans for a rising the next day.[15]

On Easter Monday, 24 April 1916, MacDonagh signed the order for the Dublin Brigade to mobilise. The 2nd Battalion, numbering no more than 150 men, assembled at St Stephen's Green and MacDonagh marched the Volunteers to Jacob's biscuit factory on nearby Bishop Street. Among those present was John MacBride, a veteran Fenian and last-minute recruit to the Volunteers, whom MacDonagh appointed as his second-in-command. His brother John was also on the march to Jacob's, along with Michael O'Hanrahan, battalion quartermaster. Six members of Cumann na mBan, the female auxiliary force of the Irish Volunteers, joined them. Jacob's biscuit factory was most likely chosen as a Volunteer position because of its commanding views over the city and its close proximity to Portobello Barracks.

Upon entering the building MacDonagh took over the clerk's office as his headquarters. Volunteers were sent to seize outposts and build barricades in the nearby streets. Throughout the day local women, who relied on the government allowances paid to them while their husbands were fighting with the British Army, shouted abuse at the Volunteers and hurled objects in their direction.

At around 3 p.m. that day, a military detachment from Portobello Barracks marched down Camden Street. On reaching Bishop Street they were fired on by the Volunteers at Jacob's. On Easter Monday evening MacDonagh ordered the withdrawal of the men from the outposts close to Jacob's, regarding them as no longer of strategic importance. MacDonagh addressed the garrison that night, as Seosamh de Brún remembered:

> In picturesque language, of which he was master, he gave an account of the Rising as it developed during the day, of the reinforcements marching to our aid from outlying districts, of allies landing on various parts of the coast, and of the reports that German submarines had formed a cordon around the country which effectually menaced any attempt on the part of the British to reinforce their Garrisons with the aid of the British fleet.[16]

MacDonagh's account of the rebellion so far, although inaccurate and misguided, lifted the spirits of the garrison. But their enthusiasm was soon quashed by the long period of inaction that followed. The incident involving the military detachment on Bishop Street on Monday proved to be the first and only serious action seen by the Jacob's garrison. British forces avoided launching an assault on the outpost for the duration of the rebellion. Situated beside tenement buildings and surrounded by a network of narrow streets, the factory was deemed unsuitable for attack. Instead, a form of psychological warfare was used against the Volunteers, where sniping during the night ensured that members of the garrison were deprived of sleep. MacDonagh appears to have been out of his depth as a military leader and more often than not it was MacBride who gave orders to the men and made decisions on military strategy.

From their vantage point in the towers of Jacob's, the Volunteers were aware of fires burning around the city. Yet, when it came, the order to surrender was greeted by the garrison with shock and disbelief. When Elizabeth O'Farrell delivered news of the surrender on Sunday morning, 30 April, MacDonagh refused to entertain her, as she was a prisoner, and insisted instead on arranging a meeting with Brigadier General Lowe. At 3 p.m. MacDonagh met Lowe at nearby St Patrick's Park and agreed to go to Éamonn Ceannt, who was in command at the South Dublin Union, to inform him of the surrender. On his return to Jacob's MacDonagh delivered the news of the surrender to his own garrison. He 'broke down and sobbed bitterly as did many of the officers and men'.[17] Some of the men refused to surrender and vowed to continue to fight on. But as the reality of the situation sank in, others put on civilian clothing and escaped from the factory. At around 5 p.m. the remaining garrison, hungry, emotional and exhausted, walked to St Patrick's Park, where MacDonagh formally surrendered.

MacDonagh was court-martialled on the same day as Patrick Pearse and Thomas Clarke, 2 May 1916. The main prosecution witness was Major J. A. Armstrong, who was also called as witness in the court martials of the other leaders who surrendered at St Patrick's Park: Ceannt, MacBride, O'Hanrahan and Con Colbert. He gave similar evidence in each case, stating that British troops in the park were fired on by snipers coming from the direction of Jacob's biscuit factory. In this trial, he testified that MacDonagh informed him he was a commandant. MacDonagh cross-examined the witness but did not call any witnesses in his defence. In June 1916 a document purporting to be an address made by MacDonagh to his court martial was published in Dublin. Around 12,000 copies of the document were published and four people were prosecuted under the Defence of the Realm Act. Doubts surround the authenticity of the document, although it is written in a style similar to that of MacDonagh. The address contains MacDonagh's declaration of 'pride and joy' at the prospect of dying for his country. He defended the inevitable failure of the rebellion by stating that 'there is always a chance of success for the brave men who challenge fortune'.[18]

The sentence of death by firing squad was passed and MacDonagh was transferred to Kilmainham Gaol on 2 May. There he wrote a statement in which he outlined his financial affairs and admitted that in relation to his family he had 'devoted myself too much to national work and too little to the making of money to leave them in competence'.[19] The same military car that failed in its attempt to reach Margaret Pearse in Rathfarnham to bring her to Kilmainham Gaol to see her son also failed to reach Muriel MacDonagh in Ranelagh to bring her to see her husband. Sniper fire prevented the car from reaching her and Thomas MacDonagh died without saying goodbye to his wife in person. One of MacDonagh's sisters, Sr Francesca, did succeed in making it to the prison and in her final moments with her brother in his cell she asked him for a lock of his hair. Her hands were shaking so much that the solider present in the cell had to cut the lock for her.

During his final hours Thomas MacDonagh received the last rites from Fr Aloysius. He was executed at around 3.30 a.m. that morning. Tragically his wife, Muriel, died in a swimming accident off the coast of Skerries, Co. Dublin, in July 1917, leaving their young children, Donagh and Barbara, as orphans.

EDWARD DALY

John Edward Daly (known as Ned) was born into perhaps the most republican family in Ireland, on 25 February 1891. The Dalys of Limerick were well known for their involvement in the IRB. His father, Edward, had been imprisoned for his IRB activities in 1866 but was released in time to participate in the Fenian Rising of 1867. He died as a result of a heart condition six months before Ned was born. His uncle John Daly had been one of the principal organisers of the IRB and at the time of Ned's birth he was serving a life sentence in Portland Prison, England. He had been convicted of treason felony for possession of explosives at Wolverhampton train station.

Ned Daly was the youngest of nine children and the only son born to his mother, Catherine (née O'Mara), a native of Ballingarry, Co. Limerick. The death of his father left the family in financial difficulty and a fund was set up locally to support them, which helped them to buy a pub on Shannon Street in Limerick city. The business failed, but the family were rescued from hardship by the return from Australia of Ned's uncle James Daly, who purchased a house for them. Known as Clonlong, the house has been described as a 'large two-storey house with extensive grounds on the Tipperary Road'.[1] Ned attended the Christian Brothers school on Roxborough Road in the south of the city. He was not a bright student and it was said that he showed 'an aversion to school life in general'.[2]

In 1896 Ned's uncle John secured his release from prison on health grounds, after a long campaign by the Amnesty Association. A crowd of 20,000 greeted him on his arrival home to Limerick. Donations presented to him in Ireland and during a speaking tour of America enabled him to open a bakery at 26 William Street in the summer of 1898. The following year John Daly was elected mayor of Limerick.

At the age of fifteen Ned began attending Leamy's Commercial School with the intention of learning the business skills needed to eventually take over his uncle's business. He then left for Glasgow where he learned bakery skills at a technical college. On his return to Limerick he was refused admission to the Limerick Bakers' Society on the grounds that his father had not been a baker. Ned's relations with his uncle John were strained, and after a bitter argument with him in 1913 he left for Dublin. As his biographer notes of his situation at this time:

> The young Ned Daly, escaping from his uncle's disapproval and the limited opportunities for employment in Limerick, had by now come of age and must have wanted to start making his own way.[3]

Daly had shown a strong interest in the military but, given his family's republican past, there was no possibility of him joining the British Army. The move to Dublin provided new opportunities for a frustrated young man.

On arrival in Dublin, Daly stayed with his sister Kathleen, the wife of Thomas Clarke. He was living in a house that was no less republican in its politics than the one he had left. Living with the Clarkes brought Daly into contact with his brother-in-law's republican associates, including Seán Mac Diarmada. Daly worked for a building contractors and a wholesale chemist, but a turning point in his life came with the foundation of the Irish Volunteers in November 1913, which provided him with an outlet for his enthusiasm for soldiering. Kathleen Clarke recalled her brother's joy on his return from the Rotunda Rink having become a member of the Irish Volunteers: 'I never saw a happier young man than he was the night he joined. He told me it was what he had always been wishing for.'[4]

Daly joined B Company, 1st Battalion and his dedication and family credentials led to his promotion to captain and later to the rank of commandant. Daly was absorbed by his activities with the Irish Volunteers and when he was not out drilling with them he was reading military manuals.

Daly was present in Howth for the landing of arms for the Irish Volunteers from Erskine Childers' yacht, the *Asgard*. Returning to his sister's house, exhausted after a day of transporting weapons around Dublin, he described to Kathleen an encounter with a group of British soldiers. On their way back to Dublin the Volunteers spotted a party of officers at the junction of Howth Road. Ned decided to proceed ahead of the Volunteers and speak with the soldiers so as to distract them. In the meantime all Volunteers approaching the junction were given word to clear away. According to Kathleen, 'the ruse worked so well that when the attention of the officer who was parleying with Ned was drawn to what was happening … very few Volunteers were left'.[5]

When the subsequent split occurred in the Irish Volunteers, Daly addressed each company of the 1st Battalion in an effort to persuade them to remain with the organisation, but the majority left to join the Redmondite National Volunteers.

Daly's closest associate in the Irish Volunteers was Séamus O'Sullivan, adjutant of the 1st Battalion. Brighid Lyons-Thornton, a member of Cumann na mBan, recalled the striking impression made by the two young men: 'They were the nearest approach to British officers in appearance and inspired us girls with feelings of enthusiasm and caused us many heart throbs.'[6] She noted that Daly was quiet 'but very forceful'.[7] Paddy Stephenson, a member of the 1st Battalion, also remembered Daly's 'soldierly figure' and observed that he had a very 'serious-looking face'.[8] Ned Daly was a talented baritone singer and during route marches he would lead the Volunteer companies in singing 'Eileen Óg', which became the anthem of the 1st Battalion. He was a regular attendee at social events held to raise funds for the Irish Volunteers, where he was 'always the life of the gathering'.[9]

Daly participated in many key events in the run-up to the Easter Rising. He was present for an Irish Volunteers parade in Limerick in 1915, at which Patrick Pearse and Seán Mac Diarmada were also in attendance. Daly suffered the indignity of having stones, rotten vegetables and other objects thrown at him in his home city as the Volunteers came under attack from a hostile crowd. By the time of the O'Donovan Rossa funeral in August 1915, he was commandant of the 1st Battalion and he led his men in the procession.

Although he was not a member of the Supreme Council of the IRB, nor was he a member of the military committee that planned the Rising and so was unaware of the details of the plans for the rebellion, Daly did sense that a rising was imminent. According to his sister, Ned did not know about the Rising until the Wednesday before it was due to take place, when Tom Clarke informed him of the plan. By Good Friday he was informing Séamus O'Sullivan of the detailed plans for his area of command, the Four Courts on the north quays in Dublin.

On Holy Saturday Daly and O'Sullivan spent the day hurrying around Dublin ensuring that as many Volunteers as possible would turn out the next day. They stayed in the Clarence Hotel on Saturday night and on leaving the hotel on Sunday morning to attend Mass, the pair saw the *Sunday Independent* newspaper containing MacNeill's notice cancelling Volunteer manoeuvres for that day. O'Sullivan recalled that such was their state of confusion that he could not remember 'if we went to Mass at all afterwards'.[10]

Daly and O'Sullivan went to Liberty Hall, where Seán Mac Diarmada informed them that the rebellion was postponed until the next day. Late on Sunday evening Daly attended a meeting at the battalion's training centre at Colmcille Hall on Blackhall Street to finalise arrangements for Easter Monday.

The 1st Battalion assembled at Blackhall Place at 11 a.m. on Easter Monday. Only one-third of the total membership turned out. Daly, as commandant, addressed the Volunteers in Colmcille Hall and explained the reason for their mobilisation. He informed them that an Irish Republic would be declared shortly and that their duty would be to defend this republic. Any Volunteers who did not wish to participate were allowed to leave. Daly was in command of a large area of strategic importance, stretching from the Mendicity Institution on the south quays as far north as Cabra in the Dublin suburbs. The battalion companies were dispersed to various outposts, including Broadstone railway station, Monks' Bakery, the Four Courts and houses and buildings on Church Street, Brunswick Street and North King Street. Cumann na mBan established a field hospital at Father Mathew Hall on Church Street and barricades were erected throughout the area. Daly established his command position at the Convent of St John, between North King Street and North Brunswick Street. On Tuesday he moved his position to the Father Mathew Hall, 'in order to be in the centre of the Battalion zone'.[11]

Daly was involved in some of the earliest action in his command area, shooting dead a British Lancer on Easter Monday afternoon. He established communications with the GPO via couriers from Cumann na mBan and the Irish Volunteers and requested reinforcements. His main duty early in Easter Week was touring his command area and inspecting each position held by the rebels. One of his great achievements, later highlighted by James Connolly, was the taking of the Linen Hall Barracks. Daly needed to gain control of this building, as it overlooked the Volunteer outposts and it would have been disastrous for the rebels if the British Army occupied it. Lacking the numbers to take the building as an outpost, Daly set it on fire instead.

On Thursday the area of the Four Courts came under heavy attack from British forces, as units of the Sherwood Foresters Regiment began to surround the positions under Daly's command. By this time Daly had hardly slept since Monday and was beginning to look tired and haggard. Nonetheless he kept going and was a source of inspiration for his battalion members. One of his messengers to the GPO, Ignatius Callendar, observed that 'he cared nothing for himself or any hardship he endured'.[12]

On Friday Daly was forced to withdraw his headquarters position to the Four Courts and release the civilian, police and military prisoners who were being held at Father Mathew Hall. The British began to form a military cordon around the command area, and intense and fierce fighting took place on North King Street and Church Street.

On Saturday news of the surrender of Pearse and the rebels was conveyed by a local priest, Fr O'Callaghan, who was accompanied by a British officer. It was confirmed with the arrival of Elizabeth O'Farrell, who handed the surrender order to Daly. Vice-Commandant Piaras Béaslaí recalled Daly's reaction:

> He showed it to me and his eyes filled with tears. He had borne himself like a gallant soldier through the week of fighting. Again he rose to this fresh test of soldiership. He checked the murmuring of those who objected to surrender by an appeal to discipline.[13]

Daly was permitted to march to Sackville Street at the head of his party of rebels, where they surrendered.

Daly awaited his court martial in Richmond Barracks along with the other rebels. His brother-in-law, Tom Clarke, was tried the day before Daly and was awaiting his death sentence in Kilmainham Gaol in the early hours of 3 May 1916. Clarke asked to see Daly. His request was granted, but there was some difficulty bringing Daly to Kilmainham given that he was a high-profile prisoner in Richmond Barracks. Michael Soughley, a DMP sergeant stationed at Kilmainham, recalled that Daly did not arrive until after Clarke had been executed:

Daly said he would like to see him dead or alive and he was allowed to remain. When the three men [Clarke, Pearse and MacDonagh] were executed their bodies lay in an old shed in which prisoners broke stones in bad weather. Daly went out to this shed – stood to attention and saluted the remains. He then took off his cap, knelt down and prayed for some time. He put on his cap again, saluted again and returned to his escort.[14]

Daly would return to this yard the following morning for his own execution.

During his court martial two prosecution witnesses, both of whom were military officers held prisoner in the Four Courts, testified against Daly. He cross-examined both witnesses and made a statement to the court in which he explained that his reason for pleading not guilty was because he had 'no dealings with any outside forces' and claimed he had no knowledge of the rebellion until the day it began. Daly was found guilty and sentenced to death.[15] Although he had not signed the Proclamation, Daly held the rank of commandant and so Commander-in-Chief John Maxwell felt justified in confirming his death sentence.

The night before his execution his sisters Kathleen, Madge and Laura visited Daly in his cell in Kilmainham Gaol. Madge found him still wearing his Volunteer uniform and observed that he 'looked so proud and strong and noble with eyes alert and full of the fire of enthusiasm that it was hard to believe that he was a captive doomed to be shot in a few hours'. They discussed the charge brought against him during the court martial and the treatment of prisoners in the Four Courts. He gave messages for his mother, aunt and sisters and said to 'tell Uncle John I did my best'.[16]

Ned Daly was the first of four prisoners to be executed at dawn at Kilmainham Gaol on 4 May 1916. John Daly passed away following an illness just two months after Ned's execution.

WILLIAM PEARSE

William Pearse lived for much of his life in the shadow of his older brother, Patrick. The pair were inseparable, and tragically Willie paid the ultimate price for this close relationship. Known as Willie to his family and friends, William Pearse was born on 15 November 1881, almost exactly two years after the birth of Patrick. His birth was difficult for his mother, Margaret, and Willie was sent to the home and farm of his uncle Christy Brady in north Dublin to be nursed. Patrick remembered Willie's birth with great fondness, recalling how he told his mother that he would allow his new brother to ride his wooden horse, Dobbin, as soon as he was big enough. He later wrote of the new arrival:

> What greater thing has happened to me than the coming of that good comrade? Willy and I have been true brothers. As a boy he has been my only playmate, as a man he has been my only intimate friend.[1]

Willie was an enthusiastic participant in the imaginative games played by the Pearse children and their cousins. Patrick began writing plays at the age of nine and Willie performed in them. When they were older they often acted out extracts from Shakespeare, their favourites being *Macbeth* and *Julius Caesar*. This fostered in Willie a love of acting that he would develop as an adult.

In 1886 the Pearse family moved from Great Brunswick Street, the city-centre location of the family's stone-sculpting business, to a house at Newbridge Avenue in Sandymount. Shortly afterwards both Willie and Patrick fell ill with scarlatina and were nursed to recovery by their great-aunt Margaret Brady. According to Patrick, Margaret told them stories from Irish history about Wolfe Tone, Robert Emmet, the Young Irelanders and Fenians, and sang ballads about exile from Ireland. Decades later, in 1915, Willie recounted a childhood memory to Desmond Ryan, while he was on holidays with the brothers at Patrick's summer house in Rosmuck, Co. Galway. He told him that 'as an infant he had knelt down at his bedside at Pat's command and they had both taken an oath to live for Ireland and die for Ireland when they grew up'.[2] Patrick also referred to this story in the statement he made at his court martial following the Easter Rising. However, like his brother, Willie's advanced nationalist opinions developed late in his life. Although their English father, James, held some radical political beliefs, he was still a firm supporter of Home Rule. According to some accounts, social occasions in the Pearse household ended with the singing of 'God Save the Queen'.[3]

Willie spent the early years of his education at a private school run by Mrs Murphy at Wentworth Place and sub-sequently attended the Christian Brothers school on Westland Row. A quiet child, he seems to have been a target for bullying. His sister Mary Brighid recalled Patrick having to defend his younger brother in the schoolyard.[4] Willie was an average student but had a gift for art, which he probably inherited from his father, a stone sculptor. He left school in 1897, having completed his Intermediate Certificate, and began studying at the Dublin Metropolitan School of Art. Willie's half-brother from his father's first marriage, James Pearse Jnr, had been involved with the family stone-carving firm, Pearse and Sons, and it seemed likely that he would one day take over the business. However, James Jnr appears to have fallen out with the family, allowing Willie to take charge when his father died suddenly of a brain haemorrhage in 1900. James Pearse Snr left a large estate which was administered by Patrick and he allowed Willie to further his artistic studies by paying for him to attend classes at the School of Art in South Kensington in London and by funding trips to Paris.

Willie and Patrick ran Pearse and Sons until 1910. The business was successful and employed a number of stone carvers. Willie executed some of the work himself, including a statue, *Mater Dolorosa*, for St Andrew's Church in Westland Row. Like Patrick, Willie was a member of the Gaelic League and he showcased his artistic talent by submitting some of his pieces of sculpture to the Oireachtas, the organisation's annual cultural festival. Willie showed considerable promise but was modest enough about his artistic abilities to state in a job application for the Dublin Metropolitan School of Art that he had 'not much to boast of in awards or results of examinations'.[5] While living with his family at Leeson Park, Willie struck up a friendship with a young girl called Mabel Gorman, who was a model for many of his sculptures but died aged sixteen in 1914. Pearse and Sons was eventually dissolved as a decline in the building of churches in Ireland, combined with Patrick and Willie's involvement in the supervision of St Enda's, meant that the running of the business was no longer viable.

In 1908 Willie Pearse was appointed teacher of art when St Enda's opened at Cullenswood House in Ranelagh. As with other family members, including his mother and sister Margaret, Willie lived at Cullenswood, contributing to the homely atmosphere of the school. Desmond Ryan, a former pupil at St Enda's and later secretary to Patrick Pearse, described the role played by Willie at the school:

> He it was who made the young idea wipe its boots on the mat and keep its fork in its left hand and answer all bells promptly. He it was who managed plays and pageants and guided clumsy fingers round circles and curves in the drawing class.[6]

In his role of art teacher, Willie's best student was Patrick Tuohy, who went on to become a successful artist. His work was exhibited at the Royal Academy in London but he died in tragic circumstances in New York in 1930.

Sports, particularly Gaelic games, formed an important part of the broad curriculum at St Enda's, and Willie played hurling and handball with the boys. Like other Irish Irelanders at that time, Willie often wore a kilt and he was regularly seen about the school 'in a smock and carrying a chisel' as he continued to work on his sculpting.[7]

Between 1908 and 1910 Willie was still managing Pearse and Sons while teaching at St Enda's and it is clear that he found it difficult to juggle these positions and to dedicate time to his artistic endeavours. In the draft job application for a teaching position at the School of Art for the academic year 1910–11, Willie outlined his frustrations:

Up to the present I feel I have not been able to do justice to myself or my work – my time being too much divided between two or more places and things. I feel certain – and perhaps those instructors who know me in the school can also say as much – that if I got a fair chance to devote my undivided attention to my work in the school [Dublin Metropolitan School of Art] I would be capable of better things.[8]

Undoubtedly Willie sacrificed some of his desire to work as an artist to support his brother in his ambition to run a school and later to become a leader in the nationalist movement. After 1910, when the school relocated to the Hermitage in Rathfarnham, Willie's responsibilities at St Enda's gradually increased. When Thomas MacDonagh left to work in the National University in 1912, and as staff numbers dwindled, Willie taught more classes and took over the staging of the school plays. During Patrick's absence from St Enda's in 1915, when he was on a lecture tour of the United States, Willie was left in charge of the running of the school. This arrangement continued up until April 1916 as Patrick's focus switched towards the nationalist movement.

Teaching at St Enda's provided Willie with the opportunity to develop his skills as an actor. He performed in the many plays produced by the school, including *An Páis*, a passion play in Irish, written by Patrick and performed at the Abbey Theatre on 7 and 8 April 1911. Willie took the role of Pontius Pilate in the production. His enthusiasm for acting prompted him to set up a drama group, the Leinster Stage Society, with his younger sister Mary Brighid and his nephew Alf McGloughlin. They had some successful productions in Dublin, including their performance of four plays at the Abbey Theatre in May 1910. But their tour to Cork was not as successful. When tickets failed to sell for a production at the Cork Opera House they had to write to Patrick seeking money to pay their costs.

In May 1915 Willie played the part of Ciarán in a new play by his brother entitled *The Master*, which was performed at Hardwicke Street Hall. This venue, home of the drama company called the Irish Theatre, was run by Joseph Plunkett, Edward Martyn and Thomas MacDonagh. A month later Willie also performed at the venue in an Irish Theatre production of *Uncle Vanya* by Chekhov.

More than anything else, it was the closeness of Willie's relationship with Patrick that led to him to follow his brother into the nationalist movement. Their adult relationship was almost childlike, with the pair continuing to speak to each other in a type of baby-talk language that they had developed as young boys. In his memoirs Desmond Ryan wrote this description of Willie as Patrick's constant companion:

> They were inseparable. Sometimes you would see them passing down the Hermitage avenue at the head of their pupils, laughing, talking, striding along *en route* for an excursion or play rehearsal. Or perhaps behind the scenes in the Abbey Theatre, busy with a

Passion Play or distributing heroic gear and garb. Again, seated in their small room in the Hermitage basement in strenuous debate, where Willie scrupled not to tell Pat just what he ought to be told or contradicted him stoutly or talked till a late hour over bills and books.[9]

Like Patrick, Willie joined the Irish Volunteers upon its foundation at the Rotunda Rink meeting in November 1913. He was later appointed captain of E Company, 4th Battalion of the Dublin Brigade of the Irish Volunteers. E Company contained many past pupils of St Enda's – including Éamonn Bulfin, Frank Burke, Desmond Ryan and Joseph Sweeney – who continued to board at the Hermitage while attending university. Bulfin recalled making munitions in the basement of St Enda's under the direction of one of the teachers, Peadar Slattery, in late 1915. Willie made plaster-of-Paris moulds into which they would pour melted lead to make bullets.

Willie Pearse cannot be said to have had a significant role in the planning of the Easter Rising. Any involvement he had in the events leading up to the rebellion arose mostly out of his tendency to accompany Patrick to meetings and assist him in his roles in the Irish Volunteers and IRB. He was with Patrick throughout many important events during this period. For instance, he accompanied his brother to Rosmuck, Co. Galway, in late July 1915, where Patrick wrote his graveside oration for the funeral of O'Donovan Rossa.

On 21 March 1916 the annual celebration to mark St

Enda's Day was held at the school. However, the occasion was more muted than in previous years, as Patrick was busy with preparations for the Rising. He addressed the pupils, describing the achievements of St Enda's and remarking that 'so far as he was concerned its work was done'. The past pupils in the room sensed that this was Patrick's farewell to the school and Frank Burke observed Willie's reaction to the speech:

> I thought poor Willie Pearse looked sad and lonely as if he had a premonition of the fate that was in store for him and his beloved brother.[10]

As the Rising approached, Willie increasingly took on the role of aide-de-camp to his brother. Oscar Traynor saw him at a meeting at Irish Volunteers headquarters, assisting Patrick in removing his Volunteer coat and slouch cap before he spoke to the assembled Volunteers.[11] During Holy Week, Patrick and Willie were a regular sight travelling around the city on their bicycles. To avoid arrest, they stayed for some of the week at the home of Seán T. Ó Ceallaigh.

On the morning of Easter Monday Willie and Patrick left St Enda's for the final time, cycling from Rathfarnham to Liberty Hall. Willie was among the mixed group of Irish Volunteers and members of the ICA who marched to the GPO shortly before noon.

Those who remembered seeing Willie in the GPO during Easter Week placed him close to his brother. Éamonn Dore noted that 'Willie never left his brother's side all that week'.[12] On Wednesday of Easter Week, when the firing on the GPO intensified, Willie accompanied his brother on a visit to check positions on the roof of the GPO. According to Desmond Ryan, Willie looked out at the scene before him and said: 'A curious business. … I wonder how it will end? I know a lot of good work has been done but there is a great deal more to do.'[13]

Patrick Caldwell, a member of the Kimmage Garrison, recalled an incident on Friday of Easter Week when he was part of a group of Volunteers asked to carry a wounded rebel, Andrew Furlong, to Jervis Street Hospital. As they neared the hospital Willie Pearse caught up with them and ordered them back to the GPO. On their return they found the GPO had been evacuated and were told by Patrick to make for Henry Place. According to Caldwell, Willie was one of the last Volunteers to leave the GPO.[14]

Willie was present at the new rebel headquarters in Moore Street when the war council of Patrick Pearse, James Connolly, Thomas Clarke, Seán Mac Diarmada and Joseph Plunkett decided on surrender. Desmond Ryan later recalled seeing tears in Willie's eyes. Patrick left the house on Moore Street to walk to the junction with Sackville Street, where he surrendered to Brigadier General Lowe. This was the last time Willie saw Patrick – as he began to round up all the rebels located in various positions on Moore Street to prepare them for surrender. Seán MacEntee, a future government minister, was in a stable at the end of the street with wounded Volunteers.

He recalled meeting Willie outside the stable and receiving the news of the surrender:

> 'What!' I cried, speaking to Pearse and breaking down with emotion, 'Has it come to this?'
>
> 'It has,' Pearse replied sorrowfully, 'but we have got terms – the best possible terms. We are all to march out with arms in our hands, and no one will be detained but the leaders.'[15]

Of course Willie was incorrect about the surrender terms – Lowe had insisted on the unconditional surrender of the rebels. There is a hint of tragedy in his remarks to MacEntee, given that Willie, who had no leadership role in the rebellion, paid with his life for his part in the Easter Rising.

Having gathered the Volunteers on Moore Street, Willie marched at the head of the company carrying a white flag, bringing them to their surrender point on Sackville Street. He and the other rebels were directed to the Rotunda Rink, where they spent Saturday night in the open air. Liam Ó Briain lay next to him and described how Willie had a very disturbed night's sleep. He appeared to be dreaming that he was back in the GPO and was heard to call out 'The fire! The fire!' now and again.[16]

The rebels were brought to Richmond Barracks the following day. Those suspected of being leaders were brought into the gymnasium. Charles Saurin witnessed the moment that helped to seal Willie's fate:

Willie Pearse was sitting near us and a big, stout red-faced 'G' man asked him his name. Apparently he considered him important when he saw the officer's uniform and the yellow staff tabs on his tunic lapels. When he got the name he must have felt he had a prize and he ordered Willie Pearse over to the other side.[17]

Willie was held at the barracks while awaiting his court martial.

The following night the authorities brought Willie to nearby Kilmainham Gaol with the intention of allowing him to visit his brother, who was shortly to be executed. Unfortunately Willie and his escort were still en route to the prison when they heard shots coming from across the road. It was the sound of the firing squad that executed his brother. Willie described this distressing incident to his mother when she was permitted to visit him in his cell shortly before his own execution the following night:

O Mother! You have come. A terrible thing happened here last night. I was brought across a yard. When we came to a gate the man with me knocked, and the answer we got was: 'You are too late.' On the minute the spirit in me grew strong. I never shed a tear. There were seven men there and one officer. They had candles in their hands.[18]

Willie was brought back to Richmond Barracks and faced his court martial later that morning, 3 May 1916. The case against him is considered the weakest of all of the executed leaders of the rebellion. The historian of the 1916 court martials, Brian Barton, has described his trial as 'a travesty of justice'.[19] Willie was court-martialled along with three others and just one prosecution witness, Lieutenant S. L. King of the Royal Inniskilling Fusiliers, was called to give evidence. In relation to Willie, King stated that he 'was an officer but we do not know his rank' and that he saw him 'wearing equipment, belts and pouches'.[20] Unlike the other executed leaders, Willie pleaded guilty to the charge put to him, that he took part in an armed rebellion. But he also made a statement in his defence, saying that his only role was that of personal attaché to his brother and that he did not have command of the rebels. Nevertheless, he was found guilty and sentenced to death. The sentence was confirmed by General John Maxwell.

Willie was transferred to Kilmainham Gaol, where he was visited by his mother and sister Margaret in the early hours of the morning of 4 May. Fr Aloysius of the Capuchin Friary had travelled out to St Enda's the previous morning to inform Mrs Pearse of Patrick's death. Not knowing of Willie's impending court martial, he told her that he thought Willie would avoid execution. Mrs Pearse responded coolly:

'No,' she said, 'I believe they will put him to death, too. They were inseparable. Willie would never be happy to live without Pat.'[21]

The Pearses were permitted a short visit to Willie in his cell, where they discussed personal matters. On their way out of the prison, Margaret Jnr sought assurances from the officers that Willie would be attended by a priest before his death. Shortly after 3 a.m. Fr Augustine, a priest from the Capuchin friary on Church Street, attended to Willie in his cell. Willie Pearse was the second of the four leaders executed at Kilmainham Gaol that morning, 4 May 1916.

MICHAEL O'HANRAHAN

Michael O'Hanrahan was born in New Ross, Co. Wexford, in 1877. His parents, Richard and Mary (née Williams), had nine children, six of whom survived to adulthood. Michael was the second eldest of the children. His father, a native of Co. Wexford, was believed to have fought in the Fenian Rising in 1867. He was a cork-cutter by trade and when Michael was still a young boy the family moved to Carlow town, where

Richard O'Hanrahan established a business. They lived at 21 Tullow Street and Michael attended the local Christian Brothers national school and also received a secondary school education.

The O'Hanrahan children would have been familiar with Irish history from their Christian Brothers schooling and they were also influenced by their father, who told them rebel stories as they were growing up. This had an impact on the young Michael. Having left school he began preparing for the entrance examination to become an excise officer in the civil service. Then one day, according to his family, he came home and told his parents that he would not take the exam as it would be 'incompatible with his principles' to take a position under the British government.[1] O'Hanrahan appears to have taken up employment instead in his father's business, and in the 1901 census he listed his occupation as a cork-cutter.[2]

The Gaelic League, founded in 1893 with the purpose of reviving the Irish language, had its headquarters in Dublin, but several branches were established around the country. Michael O'Hanrahan was instrumental in establishing a branch in Carlow town in 1898 and he became branch secretary. His knowledge of the Irish language is believed to have been acquired entirely through the Gaelic League and his own study; he was known to stay up until the early hours of the morning studying his language and grammar books.[3] He organised Irish classes at the Catholic Institute and later at the Christian Brothers school on Montgomery Street, known locally as the Academy, where *céilidhe* and *feiseanna* were also held. The Gaelic League took him to Dublin in 1900, when he attended the organisation's annual congress. All of the O'Hanrahan family were enthusiasts of the Irish language and in the 1901 census the six children claimed to be bilingual in English and Irish.

Michael and his brother Henry were founder members of the Carlow Workman's Club on Brown Street in 1899, and the name of the club was inscribed in both Irish and English above the entrance. At a club meeting in 1902 Michael objected to the proposed membership of a Lieutenant J. Corcoran, on the grounds that he was a soldier in the British Army. He was outvoted and left the club in protest at the decision.

Following the death of Richard O'Hanrahan in 1903, the family moved to Dublin. According to Henry Phibbs, who knew Michael and Henry during that period, the family initially established a small cork-cutting business on the south side of the city, but they eventually settled in Phibsborough, north of the Liffey, and Henry opened an advertising business on the quays, where he printed billposters.[4] Michael found work as a proof-reader for An Chló Cumann, the publisher of books and pamphlets for the Gaelic League. His work there was not always steady: in the 1911 census he described himself as a 'reader for the press (unemployed)'.[5]

Living in Dublin gave Michael the opportunity to become involved in some of the many nationalist organisations in the city beyond the Gaelic League, including the Celtic Literary

Society. His first chance for action came with the visit of King Edward VII to Ireland in the summer of 1903. O'Hanrahan was secretary of the National Council, a committee chaired by Arthur Griffith, which aimed to protest against the royal visit. He was attracted to the ideas Griffith was developing, including dual monarchy, where Ireland would still be ruled by the British monarch but Irish MPs would withdraw from Westminster and establish an Irish parliament in Dublin, and economic self-sufficiency, where Irish people would only purchase goods produced in Ireland. Griffith's Sinn Féin organisation grew out of the National Council and Michael O'Hanrahan was involved in this movement from its beginning in 1905. He was also actively involved with the Central Branch of the Gaelic League in Dublin, organising Irish Language Week and the Language Procession on Sackville Street that took place in March each year.

O'Hanrahan's involvement with Sinn Féin and other nationalist organisations was not always easy. In the early years of the National Council and Sinn Féin, he received a hostile reception from a crowd gathered in Newry, Co. Down, when he visited the town to speak on behalf of the organisation. On another occasion Michael and Henry participated in either a Sinn Féin or Gaelic League excursion to the Hill of Tara. When they were delayed travelling back and missed the return train to Dublin, the proprietor of a hotel in Tara refused them accommodation as he 'did not approve' of the meeting they had been attending.[6]

During this period Michael contributed articles to nationalist newspapers, including *Sinn Féin* and *Nationality*. In 1914 he published a historical novel for children, *A Swordsman of the Brigade,* about the adventures of the Irish Brigade in France in the eighteenth century. His friend Henry Phibbs recalled that O'Hanrahan spent time in the National Museum studying Irish Brigade uniforms in preparation for writing the novel.[7] The book was reviewed by Thomas MacDonagh, who wrote:

> The author knows his history, and has caught the atmosphere of the time. The book is full of military adventure, with a slight love interest. It is a manly story, of a Gael, by a Gael.[8]

A second novel, *When the Normans Came*, was published posthumously in 1918 and republished in 1931 for use in primary schools. The manuscript of his third novel was destroyed during a raid on the O'Hanrahan home after the Rising.

While Michael and Henry O'Hanrahan were founding members of the Irish Volunteers in November 1913, their sisters Cis, Máire and Eily joined Cumann na mBan in 1914, after they were encouraged to do so by Michael. He was a keen supporter of the women's auxiliary wing of the Irish Volunteers and addressed their central branch on the topic of Irish heroines during the winter months preceding the Rising. Michael became quartermaster-general of the 2nd Battalion of the Dublin Volunteers in 1915. He was also a full-time employee at Volunteer headquarters, 2 Dawson Street, where he carried out clerical work. The O'Hanrahan home at 67 Connaught Street became a meeting point for republicans, and Thomas MacDonagh and Con Colbert were frequent visitors.

O'Hanrahan was heavily involved in procuring arms and ammunition for the Volunteers, and weapons were often stored in the family home. According to his sister Eily, Irish Volunteers from around the country would come to him seeking guns. Jeremiah O'Leary, an Irish Volunteer based in London, recalled meeting O'Hanrahan on Good Friday 1916, having arranged with him the delivery of a consignment of weapons. O'Hanrahan was said to have been disgusted by the small number of guns delivered and was particularly disappointed that ammunition, which was in short supply, had not been sent.[9]

During the week before the Rising O'Hanrahan was busy with preparations for a rebellion. However, he was unaware of detailed plans as he was not a very high-ranking member of the Volunteers. On the Wednesday before Easter Week Eily O'Hanrahan met Seán Mac Diarmada, Thomas MacDonagh and her brother Michael at Volunteer headquarters. They instructed her to deliver an important dispatch to Enniscorthy, Co. Wexford, most likely giving notice that a rising was imminent. Eily was confused about who she should deliver the dispatch to, but Michael told her the next morning to bring it to Seamus Doyle, the editor of the *Enniscorthy Echo*. Enniscorthy was one of the few towns outside Dublin where rebel activity took place during Easter Week.

On Holy Thursday two Volunteers, Con Keating and Charlie Monahan, stayed with the O'Hanrahans. They travelled to Co. Kerry the next day, where they were due to make contact with the German ship the *Aud*, which was laden with arms for the rebellion. The two men were involved in a drowning accident when their car drove off the pier at Ballykissane; another Irish Volunteer, Donal Sheehan, was also drowned in the same incident. According to Eily, Michael was devastated by the news: 'Mícheál was more affected by that tragedy than ever I saw him in my life.'[10]

On Easter Monday Michael and Henry O'Hanrahan assembled at St Stephen's Green with the other members of the 2nd Battalion who had turned out for the rebellion. Thomas MacDonagh was commandant, and the last-minute arrival of the veteran Fenian John MacBride ensured his appointment as second-in-command. Michael O'Hanrahan was third-in-command at Jacob's biscuit factory and his brother Henry was in charge of the supply store, which was well equipped with clothing, tobacco and other personal items. Jacob's was the least active outpost of the rebellion and was largely disregarded by the British military, which favoured the use of psychological warfare, depriving the rebels of sleep by continuously sniping at night-time.

Eily had been sent on another dispatch mission to Wexford on Easter Monday, and when she was back in Dublin on Tuesday she eventually located her brothers in Jacob's. John MacBride tried to stop her entering the factory, but she managed to gain access by climbing a ladder. On meeting Michael she gave him news of her trip to Wexford, observing that he looked 'placid'. Although she wanted to remain with the garrison at Jacob's, Michael instructed her to go home, stating that she would be more useful guarding the weapons in the house. There were tears in his eyes as she left him and the next time they met was in Michael's cell in Kilmainham Gaol.[11]

Due to their relative inactivity during Easter Week, news of the surrender of the rebels came as a shock to the garrison at Jacob's. Although many of the men opposed the surrender, they were eventually persuaded to agree to it, with the O'Hanrahans among those who argued the case for laying down arms. Bob Price, a garrison member, noted how O'Hanrahan 'in his slow, calm and reasoned tone advised surrender'.[12] When the decision had been taken, another garrison member, John McDonald, recalled seeing the brothers 'crying together, locked in each other's arms' as they realised the rebellion was over.[13]

O'Hanrahan's court martial took place early on in the court-martial proceedings, on 3 May 1916. As with other rebels from nearby outposts who had surrendered at St Patrick's Park in the Liberties area of the city, Lieutenant J. A. Armstrong gave evidence against him. He stated that O'Hanrahan was part of a body of men who arrived from the direction of Jacob's biscuit factory and that he was armed and wearing a military uniform. O'Hanrahan made a strong effort to defend himself and chose to cross-examine Armstrong, who admitted that it was not possible for him to say whether O'Hanrahan was armed in the park, but that a list had been made of unarmed men and O'Hanrahan's name was not on that list. O'Hanrahan made a final statement in his defence but to no avail. He was found guilty and sentenced to death by firing squad.

Of the fifteen men found guilty and sentenced to death on 3 May, O'Hanrahan was one of four who had their death sentences confirmed by General Maxwell.[14] He appears to have been very unlucky to be chosen for execution, as many rebels with greater involvement in the rebellion avoided the firing squad, most notably Éamon de Valera, commandant at Boland's Mills. The fact that he held a full-time job at Volunteer headquarters may have gone against him, as his position would have brought him to the attention of police intelligence. It is also noteworthy that O'Hanrahan's execution took place before the tide of public opinion turned against the executions and he may have avoided death if his court martial had taken place later.

O'Hanrahan was transferred to Kilmainham Gaol that evening. Just after the O'Hanrahan family had gone to bed, a party of British military arrived at their home. In a tragic incident of misinformation, Eily was told that she was to come to Kilmainham Gaol to visit her brother before his deportation to England. Eily brought her sister to the prison, but decided to leave her mother at home as she suspected that they were being arrested. On arrival at Kilmainham they met Kathleen Clarke, who had just been to visit her brother Ned Daly. She recalled the moment when she bluntly informed the O'Hanrahans of the fate that awaited their brother: "'Eileen," I said, "he is being sent into the next world. This is a final goodbye.'"[15]

Eily described the scene when she was finally permitted to enter her brother's cell:

> There was nothing in it, no light even, but an old bag thrown in the corner, and a bucket, no bed, no chair, no table, a place in which you would not put a dog.[16]

During their conversation they were not allowed to talk about the Rising and Eily was interrupted by the soldiers guarding the cell when she mentioned the executions of Patrick Pearse, Thomas Clarke and Thomas MacDonagh the previous day. O'Hanrahan had been writing his will and continued to do so after his sisters left. He was attended by Fr Augustine before his death, who described him as 'one of the truest and noblest characters that it has ever been my privilege to meet'.[17] He expressed his dying wish to the priest as he walked the corridor to the execution yard, asking Fr Augustine to console his mother and sisters. Michael O'Hanrahan was executed at dawn on 4 May 1916. His brother Henry was part of a group of prisoners deported to Portland Prison in England later that day.

JOSEPH PLUNKETT

Born at 26 Fitzwilliam Square, Dublin, on 21 November 1887, Joseph Plunkett came from the wealthiest background of all the leaders of the Easter Rising. The marriage of his parents, George Noble Plunkett and Josephine Cranny, was a union of two prominent families who had made their respective fortunes from building and developing property in the south Dublin suburbs.

Joseph's father was a strong nationalist and intellectual influence during his son's early life. A descendant of the martyred Saint Oliver Plunkett, George was a supporter of Charles Stewart Parnell and ran several times as an Irish Parliamentary Party candidate in parliamentary elections. He was also a renowned scholar, and Joseph grew up surrounded by his father's collections of books and artwork. His mother, Josephine, was domineering, quick-tempered and impulsive. In later years, Joseph's sister, Geraldine, recorded that their mother was frequently abusive and neglectful towards her children. Joseph contracted tuberculosis at the age of two and was plagued with bouts of pneumonia and pleurisy throughout his childhood. His illnesses were made worse by his mother's refusal to provide him with food that he could tolerate while sick, and he often went hungry.

The Plunkett family home remained at Fitzwilliam Square, but the children lived for extensive periods at a house called Charleville, in Templeogue, and at Kilternan Abbey in Co. Wicklow. Joseph Plunkett's education was even more nomadic. He was taught initially by a governess at home and then attended the Catholic University School on Leeson Street. He was a pupil for brief periods at a Marist school in the suburbs of Paris and at Belvedere College in Dublin, and he eventually attended Stonyhurst College in England for two years.

He was an intelligent child and his interests ranged widely from literature and philosophy to science and technology. Plunkett's long periods of illness allowed him to read all kinds of books and he wrote poetry from a young age. He turned the basement of the house in Kilternan into a science laboratory where he carried out chemistry experiments. Fascinated by photography, he experimented with making coloured images using Lumière plates, and while attending Stonyhurst he was elected secretary to the dark room. Geraldine recalled how her brother was also fascinated by Marconi's wireless from a young age:

> The information [on Marconi sets] was being published in weeklies and Joe made a collection of them and started building his own sets, first in Fitzwilliam Street and then in Kilternan. He kept updating them right throughout his life.[1]

This interest was later put to practical use in planning communications for the Easter Rising. Although his ill-health prevented him from engaging in much physical activity, he enjoyed dancing and was said to have been an excellent skater.

Plunkett entered Stonyhurst, a school for Catholic boys, aged nineteen. He enrolled as a 'Gentleman philosopher', following the course offered by the college as an alternative to a university education for the Catholic upper classes. He attended the college for two years and was awarded the Philosophical Essay Prize at the end of his second year. While there he was friendly with Alfred Asphar, a Maltese student who became a 'marvellous companion' for Plunkett, and he went on holiday to Malta with him.[2]

In 1911 and 1912 Plunkett travelled to Italy, Sicily and Malta and later to Algiers, hoping that a warmer climate would improve his health. While in Algiers a volume of his poems, *The Circle and the Sword*, was published. He dedicated the book to Thomas MacDonagh, who had assisted him with the preparation of the collection. Plunkett first met MacDonagh in 1910, when Plunkett's mother employed him to teach Irish to her son in preparation for the matriculation exam of the National University. Their friendship was instant. Geraldine Plunkett observed that in spite of the fact that MacDonagh was nine years older than Plunkett, 'from the beginning it was a deep, personal and important relationship for both'.[3] The pair found common ground discussing literature and debating religious matters. In the political sphere MacDonagh was influential in guiding Plunkett towards a more radical view of Irish nationalism.

MacDonagh provided Plunkett with the opportunity to take ownership of a literary journal, *The Irish Review*, founded by James Stephens, Padraic and Mary Colum, and David Houston, which ran into financial difficulties in 1913. MacDonagh arranged a meeting between Plunkett and Houston, at which Plunkett agreed to take on the debts of the journal and become its editor. At this stage Plunkett and his sister, Geraldine, were living away from the family residence and *The Irish Review* was operated from their home at 17 Marlborough Road, Donnybrook. *The Review* continued to publish articles on the themes of literature, the arts and science, but under the stewardship of Plunkett the tone of the journal became more political.

MacDonagh was heavily involved in its production and Plunkett sought new contributors, including Roger Casement.

Plunkett and MacDonagh also worked together with the dramatist Edward Martyn to establish the Irish Theatre company, to stage new and modern European plays in Dublin. Plunkett's mother supported the Irish Theatre with financial backing, and Hardwicke Street Hall, which belonged to the Plunkett family, became the theatre company's venue. The first performance was Martyn's play *The Dream Physician*, which opened in November 1914.

The 1913 Lockout in Dublin – when workers who went on strike for the right to unionise were 'locked out' by their employers – provided Plunkett with the opportunity to become politically active for the first time. Thomas Dillon, a chemistry lecturer and Geraldine Plunkett's fiancé, was honorary secretary of the Dublin Industrial Peace Committee and he appointed Plunkett as his assistant. Plunkett also commissioned James Connolly, one of the Lockout leaders, to write an article for *The Irish Review*. Josephine Plunkett held opposing views to her children Joseph and Geraldine on the rights of workers locked out of their jobs. After a bitter row at the dinner table, in a fit of temper, Josephine decided to cancel her allowance to both of them.[4]

Joseph's involvement in the politics of Irish nationalism began in earnest with the foundation of the Irish Volunteers in November 1913. Plunkett attended the meeting at the Rotunda Rink in Dublin and was elected to the Provisional

Committee of the Irish Volunteers. From this point onwards *The Irish Review* became overtly political. In the December 1913 issue Plunkett published the 'Manifesto of the Irish Volunteers', which sanctioned the use of force to defend the rights and freedoms of Irish people. An outspoken member of the Provisional Committee, Plunkett voted for a motion to allow John Redmond, the leader of the Irish Parliamentary Party, to appoint half of the members of the Volunteer executive in June 1914. But he soon became frustrated by the presence of Redmond's nominees on the executive and, according to his sister, Geraldine, this heavily influenced his decision to be sworn into the IRB in early August 1914.[5]

In 1913 Plunkett's mother had acquired the lease on Larkfield House and Mills in Kimmage. From early 1914 Larkfield became the operational base of the 4th Battalion, Dublin Brigade, of the Irish Volunteers and was the venue for their meetings, drilling practice and classes. Geraldine Plunkett moved with her brother to a cottage in Larkfield in 1914, hoping the fresh air of the Dublin countryside would benefit Joseph's worsening tuberculosis.

Plunkett's support for extreme separatist nationalism was confirmed following Redmond's Woodenbridge speech in September 1914 at the outset of the First World War, in which Redmond called on the Irish Volunteers to join Irish regiments of the British Army in the hope that Ireland would later be rewarded with Home Rule. During the subsequent split in the organisation, Plunkett sided with the minority who opposed Redmond's appeal, and he became director of military operations in the massively reduced Irish Volunteers organisation. The members of the 4th Battalion met to discuss Redmond's speech at Woodenbridge. The battalion split into groups in favour of and against Redmond's appeal, and the reduced numbers of the Irish Volunteers continued to operate from Larkfield.

The Volunteers' position was clearly outlined in another 'Manifesto to the Irish Volunteers' signed by key figures who opposed Redmond, including Eoin MacNeill, Patrick Pearse and Joseph Plunkett. Plunkett published this manifesto in 1914 in a combined September, October and November edition of *The Irish Review*, knowing that it would attract the attention of the censors. The combined issue was in fact the last issue of *The Irish Review*, in which Plunkett outlined the financial difficulties experienced by the journal and stated that the small staff had 'been working full-time and overtime … in the Irish Volunteer organisation'.[6]

In early 1915 the IRB executive decided to send Plunkett to Germany to find out whether the German government would support a revolution in Ireland. Plunkett was chosen to travel across Europe as he 'was free to leave home and knew French'. His illness could also be used as a cover for his trip, the pretext being that he was seeking a warmer climate to improve his tuberculosis.[7] Plunkett was also adept at disguise and secrecy. He grew a beard to conceal his identity, assumed the alias James Malcolm and taught a code to Geraldine by which his letters could be read. He travelled a circuitous route to Germany, from Paris to San Sebastián, across northern Spain to Barcelona, onwards to Genoa, across Italy to the German embassy in Berne, before arriving in Berlin on 20 April 1915.

In Berlin he met with Roger Casement, who had been in Germany for over a year seeking assistance for a rebellion. Over a two-month period Plunkett and Casement held infrequent meetings with German officials, which eventually culminated in a meeting with the German Chancellor Theobald Von Bethmann Hollweg. They submitted a memorandum known as the Ireland Report, which outlined a bold plan whereby a German force of 12,000 men would land at Limerick and incite a popular rebellion in the West of Ireland that would spread across the country. The German government rejected the plan, but eventually they agreed to send a consignment of weapons to Ireland shortly before the rebellion.

After arriving back in Dublin in June 1915, Plunkett kept a low profile for the summer. He attended the funeral of Jeremiah O'Donovan Rossa in August but played no major role in organising the event. At the end of that month he made a short trip to America to update Clan na Gael on the progress of efforts to secure German assistance for a rebellion. He held meetings with John Devoy in New York and Joe McGarrity in Chicago. On his return Plunkett found Larkfield bustling with activity. The Plunkett family, including his father and brothers, George and Jack, had moved into the main house. Irish Volunteers from Britain began to arrive in late 1915 and sought refuge in the Larkfield estate. In January 1916 the IRB executive decided to use Larkfield as a camp for Volunteers. Nearly one hundred Irish Volunteers, mostly from Glasgow, Liverpool and London, arrived at Larkfield up to the time of the Easter Rising. Some were on the run from the police for their involvement in an arms raid in Glasgow, some were avoiding conscription into the British Army and others came over to help with preparations for the Rising.[8] Known as the Kimmage Garrison, they turned the estate into a munitions factory, producing weaponry for the rebellion.

On 2 December 1915 Plunkett and Grace Gifford became engaged. He had known Grace for some time, as her sister Muriel was married to his close friend Thomas MacDonagh. Some time in late 1915 their friendship developed into a romantic relationship. Grace was not Plunkett's first love. For many years he was attracted to Columba O'Carroll and he wrote several poems about her, but his love went unrequited. Although Plunkett was at this point closely involved in the planning of the Easter Rising, he did not share details of his political activities with Grace. She later stated that she had 'no knowledge of any of the military side of Joe's life'.[9]

In the months before the Rising Plunkett's health continued to worsen, and by the time of the rebellion he was terminally ill with tuberculosis. As one of the original members of the IRB's Military Committee, Plunkett was at the centre of the detailed planning for the rebellion and his sick bed was covered in Ordnance Survey maps and British military handbooks.[10]

In early April Plunkett's father, a papal count, travelled to Rome, where he sought an audience with the Pope. Acting under instructions from his son, he delivered a letter on behalf of the Irish Volunteers, informing the Pope that they had a trained force of 80,000 men at their disposal and stating that 'the people, the Catholic nation, is with us'.[11]

In the week before the Rising Plunkett was mostly involved in the circulation of the controversial 'Castle Document'. It has never been conclusively proven whether the 'Castle Document' was entirely a forgery by Joseph Plunkett, or whether it was leaked by a genuine government source. The document revealed plans by the British authorities to arrest the entire leadership of the Irish Volunteers and other nationalist organisations in Dublin and to seize their offices. Plunkett's brother Jack recalled printing the document 'in many hundreds' at Larkfield in the week before the Rising.[12] The purpose of circulating the document was to raise the temperature of the Volunteers ahead of the rebellion and to convince Eoin MacNeill of the need for pre-emptive action by carrying out an uprising.

In the days before the rebellion Plunkett transferred himself from a nursing home at Mountjoy Square, where he was being cared for, to the Metropole Hotel on Sackville Street. Michael Collins – who had been working for the Plunketts as a clerk at Larkfield since late 1915 – was now acting as Plunkett's aide-de-camp. It was Collins and W. T. Brennan-Whitmore who brought Plunkett to Liberty Hall on Easter Monday 1916. Joe Good recalled seeing Plunkett standing outside Liberty Hall holding plans for the rebellion: 'He was beautifully dressed, having high tan leather boots, spurs, pince-nez and looked like any British brass hat staff officer. Connolly looked drab beside him in a bottle green thin serge uniform.'[13] Plunkett marched to the GPO with the main body of Volunteers, which included the Kimmage Garrison commanded by his brother George.

Due to his illness, Plunkett did not play a significant military role in the GPO during Easter Week. Desmond FitzGerald, who had conversations with Plunkett in the post office on topics that varied from literature to his trip to Germany on behalf of the IRB, recalled that Plunkett looked 'appallingly ill but at the same time very cheerful'.[14] This cheerfulness may have been an indicator of Plunkett's heightened state of emotion. On Thursday, as parts of Sackville Street began to go up in flames, Plunkett was heard to exclaim joyfully that: 'It's the first time this has happened since Moscow! The first time a capital city has burned since 1812!'[15]

Plunkett's very presence in the post office, battling on in spite of his illness, provided inspiration for the rebels right up until the evacuation on Friday. He led a group from the GPO and ensured that they made it safely to Moore Street in spite of coming under heavy machine-gun fire.

On Saturday morning Plunkett was present at the meeting of the leaders at which they decided to negotiate a surrender. Shortly before or after this meeting, Plunkett wrote a letter to Grace Gifford, stating: 'This is just a little note to say I love you and to tell you that I did everything I could to arrange for us to meet and get married but that it was impossible.'[16] Plunkett had intended to marry Grace – who had converted to Catholicism early in April – on Easter Sunday 1916. But his involvement with the uprising stopped the wedding from taking place. Before the Rising began, Plunkett willed all his possessions to her.

Along with Willie Pearse, Plunkett led the surrender of the rebels at Moore Street. He spent Saturday night in the open air at the Rotunda Gardens and was transferred to Richmond Barracks the following morning. The experiences of Easter Week had taken their toll on his already poor health and Julia Grenan witnessed him 'collapse from sheer exhaustion' outside the barracks. He had to be carried inside.[17]

Plunkett's brothers, George and Jack, were held with him in Richmond Barracks. Both were court-martialled and given prison sentences to be served in England. Joseph's court martial took place on 3 May, with Colonel Maconchy presiding. Two of the prosecution witnesses were members of the British military and they testified to having seen Plunkett surrender with the other rebels on Saturday 29 April. One of the witnesses, an officer in the DMP, gave evidence that Plunkett was a signatory of the Proclamation 'issued by the Irish Volunteers'. Plunkett cross-examined this witness, questioning his knowledge as to whether or not the Proclamation was issued by the Volunteers. In his defence statement Plunkett claimed that the Proclamation 'was signed by persons who are not connected with the Irish Volunteers'.[18]

Despite this, it was Plunkett's signature on the Proclamation that ensured a guilty verdict and the confirmation of his death sentence. Shortly after his court martial he was standing in the square of the barracks when he caught sight of his father, who had been arrested a few days earlier and was being held in a separate area of the barracks. According to Geraldine, 'they gazed at each other for about half-an-hour before Joe was moved off'.[19] Plunkett was brought to Kilmainham Gaol on the evening of 3 May under military escort.

According to Grace Gifford's own account, on learning of the executions of Thomas MacDonagh and Patrick Pearse, she had a sudden premonition that Plunkett's execution was about to take place. Determined to marry him before his death, that morning she obtained marriage papers from a priest and a wedding ring from a jeweller's on South King Street.[20] The exact circumstances by which she was granted permission to marry Plunkett are not known. But their wedding ceremony did take place in the Catholic chapel of Kilmainham Gaol at approximately 8 p.m. on 3 May. Neither Joseph nor Grace was permitted to speak to the other during the ceremony, except to state their wedding vows. Plunkett was wearing handcuffs. When the ceremony was over, Grace was ordered to leave the prison immediately, but she was allowed to return later that evening to say a final goodbye to her new husband. The story of this tragic wedding had a powerful impact in turning the tide of public opinion against the executions of the rebel leaders of the Easter Rising.

Joseph Plunkett was the last of four rebels to be executed in the Stonebreakers' Yard of Kilmainham Gaol on 4 May 1916. A devout Catholic his whole life, in his final moments Plunkett was attended to by Fr Sebastian, a Capuchin priest, and he also spoke with Fr Albert and Fr Augustine. Fr Augustine recalled Plunkett's final moments:

> He was absolutely calm, as cool and self-possessed as if he looked on what was passing and found it good. No fine talk. No heroics. A distinguished tranquillity – that came from his nobility of soul and his faith – nothing more.[21]

John MacBride

John MacBride, an accidental participant in the Easter Rising, was born in Westport, Co. Mayo, on 8 May 1868. His father, Patrick, was an Ulster-Scots Protestant from Glenhesk, Co. Antrim. Patrick's merchant shipping business brought him to Westport, where he met a local woman, Honora Gill. Following their marriage they ran a shop on the quays in Westport. John was the youngest of their five sons and was educated by the Christian Brothers in Castlebar and later at St Malachy's College, Belfast. He worked for some time in a drapery business in Castlerea, Co. Roscommon, and later found employment with Hugh Moore and Company, wholesale druggists and grocers in Dublin.

MacBride was an impressionable young man when, in the late 1870s, the Land League movement swept across Co. Mayo. The Irish National Land League was founded in nearby Castlebar and the subsequent Land War, during which tenant farmers refused to pay rents and resisted evictions, was at its most intense in the West of Ireland. MacBride is believed to have been present at a 'monster' meeting held in Westport in June 1879, where Charles Stewart Parnell, the leader of the Irish Parliamentary Party at Westminster, spoke alongside Michael Davitt, the leading campaigner for tenant farmers and a member of the IRB.[1] Just four years later MacBride himself joined the IRB, later recording this event in his draft autobiography: 'when 15 years of age I took an oath to [do] my best to establish a free and independent Irish Nation'.[2]

Following his move to Dublin, MacBride's involvement with the nationalist movement intensified. In 1891 he attended the funeral of Charles Stewart Parnell as a member of the GAA, forming a guard of honour of men holding hurling sticks draped in black cloth. He attended meetings of nationalist debating clubs, including the Young Ireland Society and the Leinster Literary Society, where he met the poet W. B. Yeats, the Fenian John O'Leary and the young political activists Arthur Griffith and William Rooney. In 1896 MacBride travelled to Chicago to attend the Irish National Alliance Convention as an Irish delegate and member of the IRB. On his return, MacBride described himself as 'the most protected man in Ireland' as everywhere he went he was followed by detectives tracking his movements.[3]

Meanwhile events were occurring thousands of miles away in South Africa that would later bring MacBride to national prominence in Ireland. Tensions had existed for some time between the British living in the colonies of Natal and Cape Colony and the Boers (old Dutch settlers) living in the area known as the Transvaal. On 31 December 1895 the British colonial politician Dr Leander Starr Jameson led a group of 800 mounted policemen in a raid on the Transvaal, which ended in disaster when the Boers ambushed the raiders at Krugersdorf. The incident caused international outrage. According to MacBride, it prompted him to leave Ireland:

> Shortly after the Jameson Raid I resolved to go to the South African Republic, as I knew then England had her mind made up to take the country, and I wanted to organise my countrymen there so as to be in a position to strike a blow at England's power abroad when we could not unfortunately do so at home.[4]

MacBride moved to South Africa in 1896 and began working at the Langlaagte gold mine near Johannesburg. He held meetings to raise support among the Irish living in South

Africa for the protection of Boer independence and organised a parade in Johannesburg on 15 August 1898 to mark the centenary of the 1798 rebellion, with prominent Boer politicians in attendance. In anticipation of the outbreak of war, MacBride helped to raise an Irish brigade of 300 men to fight with the Boers against the British Army in South Africa, which included battalions of Irish soldiers. On 1 October 1899 MacBride was made second-in-command of the newly formed brigade and given the title of major.

The Second Boer War started on 11 October 1899. The Irish Brigade moved south and first saw action during the Battle of Ladysmith on 30 October. They endured fierce fighting. Three members of the brigade were killed and many were wounded. But the Irish men fought bravely and MacBride later recorded that 'the conduct of the brigade that day won the admiration of the whole Boer army'.[5] MacBride was also involved in battles at Tugela and Colenso, where a shell killed his horse and he was thrown off.

In Dublin the Irish Transvaal Committee had been set up to support the Boers and it raised support for what had become known as MacBride's Brigade. The committee sent out a green poplin flag embroidered with a gold harp to the brigade, which MacBride kept until his death. He was put forward by the Irish Transvaal Committee as a candidate for South Mayo during a by-election in February 1900 brought about by the resignation of Michael Davitt over the House of Commons' support for the Boer War. He suffered a heavy defeat at the hands of the Irish Parliamentary Party candidate, however. Meanwhile in South Africa, after a series of defeats the Boers were on the retreat and many members of the Irish Brigade deserted. The brigade disbanded in September 1900 and the Boer government chartered a steamship to transport the remaining members to Trieste.

MacBride arrived in Paris in early 1900, where he was welcomed by Arthur Griffith and Maud Gonne, a wealthy heiress of English parentage who had spent much of her childhood in Ireland, where her father had served in the British Army. She adopted many Irish nationalist causes and was a prominent member of the Irish Transvaal Committee. MacBride was unable to return to Ireland for fear of arrest and, in need of an income, he decided to embark on a speaking tour of the USA. However, he was not a natural public speaker and shortly after his arrival in New York he wrote to Maud Gonne, requesting that she accompany him on the rest of the tour. She duly travelled with him to Boston, Philadelphia, St Louis, Chicago and San Francisco, tutoring him on how to address the large audiences that turned out to hear him speak.

Maud Gonne and John MacBride were an unlikely pairing. Her upbringing was one of wealth and privilege, while he came from a modest background and had no steady income following his return from the USA. Gonne was renowned for her beauty and elegance; by contrast, MacBride, a short man with red hair and a long nose, looked worn after his adventure in the Transvaal and was known to drink heavily. Yet Gonne seems to have been attracted to MacBride's dedication to Irish nationalism and she eventually accepted his proposal of marriage. The wedding took place against the advice of their friends on 21 February 1903 at the Church of Saint-Honoré d'Eylau in Paris. Gonne had converted to Catholicism some months beforehand. Their son, Seán (who was later a founder member of Amnesty International), was born on 26 January 1904.

Almost from the time of their honeymoon the marriage of MacBride and Gonne showed signs of strain. Gonne was frequently absent from their home in Paris, and in the meantime MacBride's drinking escalated. She filed for divorce in January 1905, citing cruelty, infidelity and alcoholism. The bitter court battle took place in Paris, but was widely reported in the Irish press, tarnishing MacBride's reputation at home. The subsequent separation left MacBride an embittered man. He described his marriage to Gonne as 'the greatest and most unfortunate' of all the sacrifices he made for Ireland.[6]

MacBride returned to Dublin in 1906 and looked for work as a journalist. *The Freeman's Journal* published a series of articles containing his account of his experiences in the Boer War. He eventually obtained more secure employment with Dublin Corporation in 1911, when he was appointed to the position of water bailiff. He was at times a sorry figure, forced to keep a low profile in Fenian circles because of his damaged public image. He lodged with Fred Allan, an IRB member, but was left isolated following the death of his close friend John O'Leary in 1907.

MacBride's reputation as a Boer War hero was sufficiently intact for him to be elected to the Supreme Council of the IRB in 1911, but he was soon replaced by Seán Mac Diarmada, who was seen as part of a younger generation leading the IRB in a more radical direction. But MacBride remained involved in nationalist activities even if he was not at the centre of the organisation. In 1912 he spoke to the boys at Patrick Pearse's school in Rathfarnham about his experience of the Boer War. At a meeting in Cork in 1914 he spoke out against John Redmond's efforts to encourage the Irish Volunteers to join the British Army and fight in the war against Germany. He was present at the meeting held in the library of the Gaelic League on 9 September 1914, when it was decided to organise a rising while England was at war.

The circumstances through which John MacBride became involved in the Easter Rising were outlined by MacBride himself in a statement made during his court martial following the rebellion:

On the morning of Easter Monday I left my home at Glenageary with the intention of going to meet my brother who was coming to Dublin to get married. In waiting round town I went up as far as Stephen's Green and there I saw a band of Irish Volunteers. I knew some of the members personally and the Commander [Thomas MacDonagh] told me that an Irish Republic was virtually proclaimed. As he knew my rather advanced opinions and although I had no previous connections with the Irish Volunteers I considered it my duty to join them. I knew there was no chance of success, and I never advised nor influenced any other person to join. I did not even know the positions they were about to take up. I marched with them to Jacob's Factory.[7]

Therefore it is evident that MacBride was not involved in the planning of the Rising and that the rebellion probably came as a surprise to him. He certainly stood out from the Volunteers assembled at St Stephen's Green, looking dapper in his blue suit for the wedding and carrying a 'walking cane and smoking a cigar'.[8] He was appointed second-in-command by Thomas MacDonagh and marched with the men the short distance from the Green to Jacob's biscuit factory on Bishop Street. As they entered the building, an overzealous Volunteer let off his shotgun and MacBride was heard warning the Volunteers to treat their weapons carefully as he brushed the pellets from his moustache.[9] Although the Volunteers at Jacob's biscuit factory saw little action compared with other garrisons, MacBride still demonstrated the qualities of courage and leadership that he had developed during his time fighting in the Boer War. He took charge of bringing parties of Volunteers to outposts surrounding the factory and was seen leaving the factory at dawn via the lower windows on Bishop Street to conduct the rebels to their positions.[10] He won the admiration of the garrison at Jacob's. MacDonagh's brother John later noted that 'MacBride's influence was useful in steadying our men' and Seosamh de Brún admired MacBride for the 'inspiring language' he used when addressing them.[11]

It was during the surrender of the garrison that MacBride's coolness under pressure was most in evidence. Early on Sunday morning Elizabeth O'Farrell arrived at Jacob's, bringing with her the order from Pearse to surrender. MacDonagh insisted on negotiating directly with Brigadier General Lowe, whom he met at noon at St Patrick's Park. He agreed to accept the order to surrender and on his return the garrison greeted the news with consternation. MacBride intervened to calm the men, as Joseph Furlong recalled:

> Capt. Tom Hunter and some of the men kicked against surrendering and wanted to continue the fight, but McBride [*sic*] asked them did they think he would surrender if he thought there was any chance of success, adding, that we must now save the lives of our people. This had the effect he wanted, and we all agreed.[12]

MacBride also suggested to the men and women present that they should take the opportunity to escape. However, he himself remained with the garrison, insisting that he would not leave his men. MacBride stood alongside MacDonagh as they marched the men to the surrender point at St Patrick's Park.

MacBride's court martial took place on 4 May 1916. Three

prosecution witnesses were called and the evidence brought against him included his presence at St Patrick's Park on Sunday evening, his use of the title 'Major' when giving his name to the lieutenant who searched him in the gymnasium at Richmond Barracks and the fact that he was found in possession of incriminating documents. MacBride called his landlady, Mrs Allan, in his defence and she corroborated his statement that he happened upon the Rising by accident while on his way to meet his brother. MacBride was found guilty and sentenced to death. His death sentence was confirmed that evening. It is worthy of note that both Brigadier General Blackader, who presided at MacBride's court martial, and General Maxwell, who confirmed his death sentence, had served during the Boer War. Although it cannot be proven decisively, these men may have harboured some resentment towards MacBride for fighting with the Boers, and that possibly influenced their decisions.

MacBride was transferred to Kilmainham Gaol on the evening of 4 May and at 2 a.m. the next morning Fr Augustine was called to the prison to attend to him before his execution. He made his confession and gave Fr Augustine a set of rosary beads to give to his mother. MacBride requested that his hands would not be tied during his execution and that he could face the firing squad without a blindfold. Both requests were refused. He turned to the priest and said: 'You know, Fr Augustine, I've often looked down their guns before.'[13] John MacBride was executed at 3.47 a.m. on 5 May 1916.

Maud Gonne learned of the news of MacBride's death when she read about it in a newspaper while holidaying in Normandy.

SEÁN HEUSTON

John Joseph Heuston (known as Seán) was born in Dublin on 21 February 1891. His family lived at 24 Gloucester Street and later moved to Jervis Street. Both of these areas of the north inner city contained mostly tenement dwellings.[1] At the time of his birth Heuston's father, John, was employed as a clerk. It appears that he was no longer living with the family by the time Seán was ten years old. According to the 1901 census,

Seán Heuston, his mother, Maria, sisters Mary and Teresa, and brother Michael were living at 34 Jervis Street with Maria's sisters, Teresa and Brigid MacDonald.[2] Little is known as to the whereabouts of John Heuston at this time. All that is certain is that by the time of the Easter Rising he was living in London and that Seán Heuston's final letter to his father hints at a strained relationship between John and the rest of the family.

Heuston was educated by the Christian Brothers and was a bright student. He learned Irish at school and was the only one of his siblings to list his ability to speak the language on the 1901 census. In 1905 he completed the Intermediate Certificate and in 1907 he took examinations for clerical positions at the Great Southern and Western Railway Company (GSWR). In spite of the large number of applications for these secure and reasonably well-paid jobs, Heuston was successful. He was appointed as a clerk at the GSWR offices in Limerick, where he worked until 1913. According to reports of his employers, Heuston was a satisfactory worker, described as having 'good habits generally'.[3]

Heuston's time in Limerick coincided with the spread of the nationalist youth organisation Na Fianna Éireann across Ireland. The organisation was established in Dublin at a meeting in Camden Hall organised by Bulmer Hobson and Constance Markievicz. Markievicz visited Limerick in the summer of 1911 to set up a Fianna Éireann branch, or *sluagh*, in the city. Seán Heuston was the driving force behind the organisation of the Limerick *sluagh* and he trained the young boys in military drill and other skills.[4] Madge Daly, of the renowned republican family in Limerick, recalled Heuston's contribution to Na Fianna Éireann in the city:

> With all he was most practical, and had the special quality for managing boys and getting the best from them. A fluent Irish speaker, Seán used his own language whenever possible. He was methodical, and planned each year's Fianna programme in advance, arranging classes, lectures, marches and examination for the boys ...[5]

Heuston's practical approach to running the Fianna in Limerick extended to setting up a payment scheme so that members who could not afford to pay upfront for uniforms and equipment could instead make weekly contributions to pay for them. This ensured that Fianna members were well turned out for drilling practice and parades. As well as the usual Fianna activities of drilling, scout training, signalling and musketry, Heuston also placed an emphasis on Irish history and language classes. Daly noted that Heuston was 'educated to an exceptional degree in subjects relating to his country'.[6]

Heuston's involvement with the Fianna brought him into contact with important individuals in the republican movement. John Daly, who had been imprisoned in England for his Fenian activities, provided money and a plot of land on Limerick's Barrington Street for the construction of a hall for the organisation. Bulmer Hobson gave a lecture to the Fianna on the occasion of the opening of the building. Seán Mac Diarmada and Tom Clarke were regular visitors to the hall. Heuston also travelled to Dublin, where he met other Fianna members at the annual meetings of the organisation, known as *ard fheiseanna*.

In 1911 Heuston was a founding member of the Wolfe Tone Club in Limerick. This organisation was essentially a front for the IRB, so Heuston was a member of the underground organisation aged just twenty.[7] According to one of its members, Patrick Whelan, members paid subscriptions for the purchase of rifles, which were distributed to IRB centres in Limerick. By 1912 Heuston was actively recruiting for the IRB in Limerick, when he discussed with Patrick Whelan his attitude to joining a secret society.[8]

In autumn 1913 Heuston's time in Limerick came to an abrupt end when he was relocated to Dublin by the GSWR. He quickly became involved in Fianna activities in the city, drilling members at the Dun Emer Guild on Hardwicke Street. Seán Prendergast recalled his first impression of their new officer:

From the first Seán captivated the hearts and won the affections of us all, which was not surprising when one considers that he was endowed with a pleasant, easy and simple nature, a bright and lovable disposition which, coupled with his natural understanding of boys, made such ready appeal to us.[9]

Heuston owned many military books and training manuals and spent his spare time studying them. His military knowledge may have been what inspired him to design a special trek cart, used by the Fianna *sluagh* to transport their camping, first aid and signalling equipment. The trek cart was later put to use during the Howth gun-running, when it was used to transport weapons to the city centre.

Heuston's military skills were also put to use in other organisations within the republican movement. He drilled members of the IRB at the National Forrester's Hall, including a number of older students from Patrick Pearse's school, St Enda's. Heuston and another leading member of the Fianna, Con Colbert, had come to know the St Enda's boys from drill practice led by the two men at the school in Rathfarnham. On the foundation of the Irish Volunteers in November 1913, Heuston became captain of D Company, 1st Battalion, Dublin Brigade. D Company met at Colmcille Hall at Blackhall Street in the north inner city.

Fianna members, directed by Seán Heuston, played a very active role in the landing of arms at Howth. Senior Fianna boys were handpicked to participate and they gathered at the Dun Emer Guild on the morning of 26 July 1914. They marched to Father Mathew Park in Fairview, where they met with groups of Volunteers and marched onwards to Howth village. Prendergast recalled seeing Heuston in 'deep and earnest conversation with Bulmer Hobson'. Heuston then ordered Prendergast and another Fianna member to run along the pier and to signal with their bugles if they saw a white yacht. They spotted the *Asgard* and shortly afterwards the yacht's cargo of arms was unloaded onto the pier. Prendergast described the scene:

> Our group of Fianna boys, with our trek-cart, were assembled in direct proximity to the yacht, receiving the rifles and passing them along the lines of Volunteers that stretched along the pier in human chain fashion to receive them. Another group commanded by Seán Heuston were loading the trek-cart with boxes. Some Volunteers were loading motor cars that had come on the scene. With willing hands, eager and willing to work hard, the task of unloading was quickly accomplished …[10]

On their return to Dublin, the Fianna boys encountered a party of British military approaching the Howth Road from the direction of the Malahide Road, and Heuston ordered the boys to retreat from the road to a nearby field. In the meantime Heuston procured a lorry to transport the arms back to Dublin.

Heuston was not directly involved in the planning of the Easter Rising. One of his main activities in the months before the rebellion was obtaining weapons for the Irish Volunteers. Paddy Stephenson, a member of Heuston's D Company, recalled one particularly brazen incident of arms procurement. Heuston asked Stephenson to accompany him to Broadstone Station, where they found a party of British soldiers disembarking from a train. They left their rifles leaning against the platform wall while they went to the station café. Heuston marched confidently up the platform and took one of the rifles and hid it under his coat.[11]

It is uncertain when exactly Heuston became aware of the date of the rebellion. While awaiting execution in Kilmainham Gaol, he was asked by his brother if he knew in advance that the Rising would take place. He replied:

> I had strong suspicions for about a week before, as we were moving stuff everywhere. We moved a cart-load from a house on Prussia Street on Good Friday. I was almost certain from then on but got no definite order till Easter Monday morning.[12]

Heuston spent the days preceding the Rising in and around the headquarters of D Company at Colmcille Hall. On hearing of Eoin MacNeill's countermanding order on Easter Sunday, he went to Liberty Hall to receive instructions from the other leaders. From there he was sent with his company quartermaster, Michael Staines, to see Éamon de Valera, commandant of the 3rd Battalion, and inform him of the cancellation of Volunteer manoeuvres. On receipt of the order, de Valera threatened to arrest Staines and he refused to say whether or not he would obey the order. According to Staines, Heuston was indignant at de Valera's attitude and told Staines 'he was almost on the point of drawing his gun'.[13]

Heuston spent the night before the Rising guarding

the large stores of ammunition in Colmcille Hall. The next morning D Company assembled outside St George's Church on Temple Street in the north of the city. As a result of the confusion caused by MacNeill's countermanding order, they were significantly undermanned, with just eleven of the thirty-six members present. Stephenson recalled how the men could not help but smile at Heuston's appearance as he looked 'ridiculous' in a Fianna hat that was 'a size too small for his head'.[14] He marched the company to Liberty Hall, where he received instructions from James Connolly to seize the Mendicity Institution. The Mendicity, a large building situated on the south quays of the River Liffey, opposite the Royal (now Collins) Barracks, provided food and shelter for the destitute in Dublin. The purpose of taking the building was probably to delay troops in the Royal Barracks opposite from attacking the Four Courts, which was soon occupied by the other companies of the 1st Battalion.

The rebels seized the Mendicity Institution and the occupants were hurried out at gunpoint. The Volunteers began smashing windows and barricading them with whatever furniture they could find. One of the company, Seán McLoughlin, threatened a group of people standing on Bridge Street by drawing his revolver, and they helped him to erect a barrier on the street by pulling carts across the road. Minutes later the Mendicity garrison saw its first action with the approach of a party of approximately thirty soldiers on the opposite side of the quay. The soldiers were unarmed and Heuston instructed his men to 'fire over their heads and scatter them and give them a scare'.[15]

After this incident the garrison at the Mendicity Institution was left mostly undisturbed by the British military until Wednesday. McLoughlin brought messages to and from the GPO, obtained food supplies from a local public house and went to Heuston's home to retrieve ammunition and destroy incriminating documents. Twelve Volunteers from the Fingal Brigade reinforced the garrison. Heuston carried out regular inspections of their position, organised a sleeping roster for night-time duty and provided words of encouragement to boost the morale of his men.

On Wednesday morning the Mendicity came under fierce attack from enemy forces. The building was completely surrounded by the Royal Dublin Fusiliers, who had approached the building via back streets and evacuated the neighbouring houses. Machine guns were placed on a nearby bridge and on the roof of the Phoenix Picture House. The garrison in the Mendicity came under heavy gunfire and grenades were hurled at the building. After less than a quarter of an hour of unrelenting attack, Heuston was left with no choice but to surrender. Heuston's brother Michael later described the moment of surrender:

Jack [Seán Heuston] threw out a white sheet, but the soldiers continued firing. He then sent out the captive soldier, but they sent him back, saying they wanted a Volunteer. Jack came to the door, put out the white flag and called out: 'Do you recognise the white flag?' They said 'yes', but he seems not to have heard and repeated the question. 'Yes,' they said, 'come out'.[16]

A British sniper fatally wounded one of the men from the Fingal Brigade, Peter Wilson, during the surrender. Heuston and the rest of the garrison were marched across the river to the Royal Barracks. The order given by Connolly to Heuston to seize the Mendicity was found on him and was later used as evidence against him in his trial. Heuston was not brought to Richmond Barracks until the day of his court martial. He was held at Arbour Hill as the Rising was still ongoing and the final surrender did not occur until the following Sunday.

Heuston's court martial took place on 4 May 1916 and was presided over by Colonel Maconchy. According to Heuston, his court martial lasted only twenty minutes and he described the state of the officers as 'dreadfully vexed because we killed so many soldiers'.[17] He was tried alongside three Volunteers who had also been taken prisoner outside the Mendicity Institution: W. O'Dea, P. Kelly and J. Crenigan. Heuston told his brother that 'we were condemned beforehand and it was only a question of fixing the sentences'.[18] Two prosecution witnesses from the Royal Dublin Fusiliers testified against them. Both witnesses identified Heuston as being present at the Mendicity. One of the witnesses, Captain MacDermot, listed a number of documents that incriminated Heuston, including the order signed by Connolly, message books signed by Heuston as

'Capt.' and copies of messages to Connolly. Another witness identified Heuston as the leader of the rebels at the Mendicity. Heuston attempted to defend himself, desperately trying to use a spelling error made by Connolly to his advantage. He claimed that because Connolly had addressed his order to a 'Captain Houston' that the order was not intended for him. His efforts were in vain and he was found guilty and sentenced to death.

Immediately after his court martial Heuston was transferred from Richmond Barracks to Kilmainham Gaol and did not learn of the confirmation of his death sentence until Sunday 7 May. He requested visits from his brother Michael, who was training to be a priest at the priory in Tallaght, his mother, his sister Teresa and his aunt Teresa MacDonald. While waiting for them he wrote to his sister Mary, a Dominican nun in Galway. He asked her to pray for him and called on her 'to teach the children in your class the history of their own land, and teach them that the cause of Caitlín Ní Uallacháin never dies'.[19]

Heuston's brother Michael left a detailed account of his final visit with Seán, during which he asked him many questions about his participation in the Rising.[20] Their mother, sister, aunt and first cousin Lil Heuston were also present. Michael found his brother in his cell 'unshaven, drawn, and dreadfully troubled looking', but Seán declared to him that he was 'quite ready to go. I am dying for Ireland.' Heuston responded to his brother's questions about events at the Mendicity, his knowledge of the Rising beforehand and his opinion of how it would be received in the country. During the visit Heuston expressed his concern for his mother, as he had been supporting her financially through his job with the GSWR. To this end he wrote to his employer asking that whatever salary and pension was owed to him be given to his mother. He also wrote to his father in London, stating that it was now 'many years' since he had written to him and informing him that he was under sentence of death. He pleaded with his father to take care of his mother:

> I have for years been my mother's main support and now I make this appeal to you from the jaws of death to assist my mother as far as lies in your power.[21]

As his family left him for the final time, Heuston uttered the words, 'Pray, pray hard for me.' Fr Albert visited him in his cell at 3.20 a.m. He remained with him until 3.45 a.m. on 8 May 1916, when Seán Heuston was taken to the Stonebreakers' Yard and executed by firing squad.

MICHAEL MALLIN

Michael Mallin was born on 1 December 1874 at Ward's Hill in the Liberties area of Dublin city. The Mallin family had lived in Dublin for some years and Michael's grandfather John Mallin owned a small boat-building yard on City Quay, which had been in the family for five generations.[1] Michael's father, John, was a boatwright and carpenter. His mother, Sarah (née Dowling), had worked in a silk factory in Macclesfield,

England, but lost her position when she expressed sympathy for the Manchester Martyrs – William Allen, Michael Larkin and Michael O'Brien – members of the IRB who were executed for causing the death of a police officer in 1867. According to her son, Sarah actually witnessed the attack on the police van that was carrying two arrested leaders of the IRB.

Sarah Dowling returned to Ireland and married John Mallin. Michael was the eldest of nine children, of whom four boys and two girls survived childhood. The family lived in a tenement building in a working-class area of Dublin city. Michael received some primary education at the local national school at Denmark Street. But like many young boys of his generation in Dublin, his schooling was short-lived as he was expected to provide for his family from a young age. His uncle James Dowling was a pay sergeant in the British Army, stationed at the Curragh, Co. Kildare. Mallin went on holidays to the Curragh when he was fifteen years old and was persuaded by his uncle's wife to enrol in the British Army as a drummer.

Mallin joined the 21st Royal Scots Fusiliers at Birr, Co. Offaly, on 21 October 1889.[2] The role of the drummer in the army was to aid communications on the battlefield, with different beats and drum rolls indicating different commands from officers. Mallin served for approximately fourteen years in the British Army, and in the early years of his service his regiment was mostly stationed in garrisons around Britain and Ireland. He learned to play other musical instruments during his army career, notably the flute, for which he had a particular talent.

In 1896 the Royal Scots Fusiliers were transferred to India, where Mallin saw out the rest of his service. He was stationed in the Punjab and saw active service during the Tirah Campaign, in an area of British India that is now modern-day Pakistan. He contracted malaria and symptoms of the illness recurred throughout his life. During his time in India Mallin was asked to make a donation to a memorial fund for Queen Victoria's jubilee year. He refused to do so, explaining 'that he could not subscribe as the English monarch had taken an oath to uphold the Protestant faith'.[3] It was incidents such as this that prevented Mallin from gaining a promotion in the army higher than the rank of drummer. According to his biographer, during his time in the British Army Mallin's political beliefs 'radicalised … and he grew to detest having to serve with the British Army'.[4] Some years later Mallin apparently told Robert de Coeur, a lieutenant in the ICA, that 'he learned his militant Irish nationalism in the hill stations of India' by observing the tactics of the tribesmen he fought against.[5] By the end of his service he was desperate to leave, but numerous delays on the part of his superiors in the army meant that he was not discharged until nearly two years after his period of service was complete.

On his return to Dublin Mallin was taken on as an apprentice by James Dowling, now retired from the British Army, who had become a silk weaver at Atkinson's poplin factory in Dublin. Silk weaving was a traditional industry in Dublin city. The fact that Mallin's mother had been a silk weaver in Manchester enabled Mallin to secure this position, as only the sons and daughters of qualified silk weavers could be taken on as apprentices.

During his period of home service with the Royal Scots Fusiliers, Mallin had met Agnes Hickey from the Chapelizod area of Dublin, whose father had participated in the Fenian uprising of 1867. While on service in India he wrote to Agnes every month without fail. They were married in Chapelizod church in 1903, after Mallin had been discharged from the army.[6] Their first son, James (known as Séamus), was born within their first year of marriage. Over the next eight years, the Mallins frequently moved to different addresses around Dublin city. Mallin put his talents as a musician to good use by giving private lessons at his home and he was musical director of a small group of musicians who performed concerts at the Antient Concert Rooms.[7] By 1911 the couple and their three children, James, John (known as Seán) and Úna, were living at 65 Meath Street, where they also kept a small shop selling sweets, tobacco and newspapers. At this point Mallin was secretary of the Silk Weavers' Union, representing the interests of the workers in the silk weaving factories.

In 1909 the Socialist Party of Ireland was reorganised under the trade unionist William O'Brien, and Mallin was appointed to a socialist unity committee aimed at healing divisions within the socialist movement in Ireland. Mallin came to prominence in trade union circles in Dublin in 1913, when he was the main organiser of a silk weavers' strike in the city. 1913 was a time of major industrial unrest and from September many workers were 'locked out' of their jobs as employers refused to allow workers to become members of trade unions. Earlier that year, in March, Mallin had led a strike of silk weavers at the Hanbury Lane factory of Atkinson's and Co. Poplin Manufacturers. The cause of the strike is uncertain, but it was probably to do with the fact that workers were paid on a piece rate and had to wait lengthy periods for materials to arrive, going without pay in the meantime.[8] The strike lasted for thirteen weeks and Mallin was active in negotiating on behalf of the striking workers, as well as writing articles explaining their case in the socialist newspaper the *Irish Worker*.

By the end of 1913 Mallin was forced to close his shop on Meath Street as he had lost a lot of his police customers because of his support for the newspaper boys during the Lockout. At this stage he seems to have contemplated emigration. His friend James O'Shea recalled that Mallin discussed 'the possibilities of getting away to Argentine [*sic*] or some South American State. He said he would never be able to stick Ireland as she was at that time.'[9] He remained in Ireland, however, and briefly moved to Finglas in the Dublin countryside where he intended to set up a chicken farm. But he contracted Bright's disease and spent whatever money he had left from the sale of the shop on medical fees, forcing him to return to the city centre.

Around this time Mallin began his association with the Inchicore branch of the Irish Transport and General Workers' Union (ITGWU) as he was the conductor of the Emmet Fife and Drum Band, which practised in Emmet Hall in Inchicore, the headquarters of the ITGWU branch run by William Partridge. When Partridge was appointed as a national organiser for the ITGWU in 1914, Mallin replaced him as head of the Inchicore branch. The family moved to Emmet Hall and opened a newsagents at the front of the building.

Mallin also set up a branch of the ICA, the military wing of the ITGWU established during the Lockout to defend workers' rights. He started out with 'just 12 or 14 men' who met twice weekly to drill in the hall and again at weekends at Croydon Park in Fairview. Upon the outbreak of the war in Europe in August 1914, the Inchicore Company decreased in size when members left to fight with the army. But this did not deter Mallin, and the smaller the company the more active he became, supplementing the drill sessions with lectures on soldiering.[10]

In late 1914, when James Larkin, the leader of the ITGWU, went to America, James Connolly was left to reorganise the trade union movement in the aftermath of the collapse of the Lockout. He appointed Mallin to the position of chief of staff of the ICA, given the military knowledge he had gained from his years of experience with the British Army. Through intensive training Connolly and Mallin shaped the ICA into a small but effective military force. James O'Shea's memory of the period was that 'it was drill, drill, most of the time'.[11] Mallin also entered the ICA into competitions, including one organised by the Ancient Order of Hibernians (AOH) in Carlow. The AOH tried to prevent the ICA from attending the drill competition by instructing railway officials at Kingsbridge Station to refuse to allow the ICA members to board the train for Carlow. Determined that the ICA would travel, Mallin instructed his men to 'fix bayonets' and to clear the train of its passengers, giving the order not to allow the train to leave the station. Eventually the staff at the train station relented and allowed the ICA to travel to Carlow, where they won first prize for drill and handling of arms.

Mallin lectured the ICA on all aspects of guerrilla and urban warfare and he published articles on these topics in *The Workers' Republic*, the newspaper of the ITGWU. He was involved in trying to procure weapons for the ICA and, as Emmet Hall was situated next to Richmond Barracks in Inchicore, Mallin persuaded some of the soldiers to give him arms. O'Shea recalled spending 'many nights with Mallin under the walls of Richmond Barracks waiting for "friendlies" to hand over stuff [weapons]'.[12] He also participated in the social aspects of the ICA, playing every Sunday as part of a quartet of musicians who gave concerts in Liberty Hall.

Mallin did not always make a strong impression as a military man. James Connolly's daughter Nora, on being told by her father that Mallin was to be chief of staff of the ICA, expressed her disbelief that a short, slight, pale and gentle person such as Mallin could really be 'a great soldier'.[13] According to ICA member John Hanratty, Mallin's 'smile and gentleness were the two characteristics that struck one most forcefully particularly on meeting him for the first time'.[14] Mallin could also come across as a very serious person. He was a devout Catholic and was involved in the temperance movement from a young age.

Similar to the other like-minded nationalists at the time, Mallin saw the outbreak of the First World War as an opportunity to strike against England. His brother remembered him pointing to a map of Europe and predicting that the British were about to take Salonika, which would make it 'a good time for a row'.[15]

From January 1916, when Connolly was co-opted onto the Military Council of the IRB, Mallin was aware that an uprising was imminent. One month before the Easter Rising, Nellie Gifford Donnelly recalled that Mallin came into the employment bureau she had set up at Volunteer headquarters on Dawson Street to tell her that the date of the Rising was 'all fixed now' for Easter Sunday 1916.[16] Holding the rank of commandant in the ICA, in the week before the Rising, Mallin gave instructions to ICA members on their duties for the rebellion.

When the Rising eventually broke out on Easter Monday, Mallin was in charge of the area around St Stephen's Green in Dublin city. At around 11.30 a.m. he departed Liberty Hall with a small force of men and women, arriving at the

Green around noon. The rebels evacuated the park, escorting away at gunpoint the men, women and children who had been enjoying the bank holiday sunshine. They began to dig trenches, establish first aid posts and kitchens, and erect barricades in the surrounding streets. One of the ICA's most prominent members, Constance Markievicz, arrived on the scene and was appointed second-in-command. In the chaos of the morning a number of civilians were shot: Michael Cavanagh was fatally wounded as he tried to retrieve his cart of theatrical props, which had been used as part of a barricade.

Mallin intended to take the Shelbourne Hotel on the northern side of St Stephen's Green but insufficient numbers prevented him from doing so. The failure to take the Shelbourne proved disastrous for the rebels. On Monday night the British military occupied the upper floors of the hotel, and in the early hours of Tuesday morning they opened fire on the rebels encamped in the park below.

Under intense machine-gun fire, Mallin ordered his garrison to retreat to the Royal College of Surgeons on the western side of the Green. The rebels barricaded the windows of the large stone building with books, furniture and other materials. The garrison remained there for the rest of the week, held under siege by sniper and machine-gun fire. Mallin sent detachments of rebels to tunnel through buildings to reach Grafton Street. Their eventual aim was to take the United Services Club, where the British military had established a machine-gun position, but they did not succeed. By Thursday the garrison was cut off from communication with the GPO and by Friday the rebels were exhausted and hungry as they witnessed dark smoke rising from the area around Sackville Street.

Mallin's strengths as a commandant during Easter Week included his strict regime of discipline at the Royal College of Surgeons, where access to the building was strictly controlled by a system of passwords and the garrison had to make and fold their beds each day.[17] He demonstrated strong leadership during the evacuation of the Green and did not leave the park until all of the rebels had reached the Royal College of Surgeons. But Mallin has been criticised by historians for his failure to take the Shelbourne Hotel and for attempting to take an open and vulnerable position such as St Stephen's Green in the first place.

The garrison at the Royal College of Surgeons were not informed of the surrender until Sunday morning, when the order was delivered to Mallin by Elizabeth O'Farrell. Having discussed the order with his officers, Mallin assembled the garrison in the lecture hall and informed them of the headquarters' decision. Frank Robbins, a garrison member, described the scene:

The whole St. Stephen's Green division was paraded into the Long Room, when Mallin read out the news and addressed a few remarks to them, followed by Madame Markievicz and William Partridge. Commdt. Mallin in the course of his address said that it was quite possible for a number of the men and women then present to go back to their homes … and nothing the worse would be thought of them for doing so.[18]

Major de Courcy Wheeler accepted the surrender of the rebels at the Royal College of Surgeons and the garrison members were taken prisoner and marched to Dublin Castle and onwards to Richmond Barracks. There, Mallin was separated from the rest of the garrison and identified for a court martial.

His court martial took place on 5 May 1916. During his trial, Mallin made a desperate effort to convince the court that he was not the commander of the St Stephen's Green garrison but rather one of the rank-and-file rebels. In his defence statement, Mallin claimed that he 'had no commission whatever in the Citizen Army' and stated that he had no knowledge of the Rising before Easter Monday.[19] He strongly implied that Markievicz was in command of the garrison by stating that she ordered him to take command of the men, when in fact the reverse was the case. Mallin was the father of a young family and his attempt to try to save his own life was understandable. In so doing, however, he placed the life of Markievicz under threat by suggesting that it was she who was in command of the garrison. Mallin was found guilty of participating in an armed rebellion and sentenced to death. He was transferred to Kilmainham Gaol that evening and his death sentence was confirmed the next day.

Mallin's family had been uncertain of his whereabouts

for much of Easter Week. His brother Thomas had searched Dublin but found no sign of him. On Wednesday Thomas brought Agnes and her youngest children to his home in Dolphin's Barn. On the night of 7 May Mallin was visited in his cell by his mother, Sarah, his pregnant wife, his four children and three of his siblings. His final letter to his wife was perhaps the most poignant and emotional of all the last letters written by the leaders of the Rising. He told Agnes that he was prepared for death but wished that his family could come with him:

> My heartstrings are torn to pieces when I think of you and them of our manly James happy go lucky John shy warm Una dadys [*sic*] Girl and oh little Joseph my little man my little man. Wife dear Wife I cannot keep the tears back when I think of him he will rest in my arms no more.[20]

In the letter Mallin expressed his dying wish that his son Joseph would become a priest and that his daughter Úna would become a nun. Joseph and Úna fulfilled their father's request in later life, becoming a Jesuit priest and Loreto nun respectively.

Michael Mallin was executed between 3.45 a.m. and 4.05 a.m. on Monday 8 May 1916.

ÉAMONN CEANNT

Éamonn Ceannt was born Edward Kent on 21 September 1881 in Co. Galway. His use of the Irish form of his name dates from his involvement with the Irish language movement in the early 1900s. His family lived in the RIC barracks in the small village of Ballymoe, located near the Co. Roscommon border, where his father, James, was a constable. The second youngest of seven children, Éamonn was just two years old when James was transferred to Ardee, Co. Louth. However, Co. Galway continued to hold a special place in Ceannt's life and he returned often to the West of Ireland on holidays in later years. Ceannt attended De La Salle national school in Ardee and later the Christian Brothers school at Sunday's Gate, when his family moved again, this time to Drogheda. When James retired from the RIC in 1892, the Ceannts finally settled at 232 Clonliffe Road, Drumcondra, Dublin. There, Éamonn was a student at the O'Connell school on North Richmond Street, paving the way for the younger revolutionaries Con Colbert and Seán Heuston who would also attend this school.

Ceannt was a shy, withdrawn young boy. His brothers recalled that he would not enter a shop to spend his pocket money, but instead gave his penny to them to buy his sweets. Much to the surprise of his father, he overcame his reserve to give the oration at an annual banquet held at the school to celebrate the students' achievement in the Intermediate Certificate examinations. Ceannt was noted as a quiet and serious man throughout his adult life; a former colleague recorded that he had 'a sullen dourness' that 'gave to his manner a sharpness and abruptness that repelled rather than attracted'.[1]

After leaving school, Ceannt successfully completed exam-inations to secure a position with the clerical staff in the City Treasurer's Office of Dublin Corporation in 1899. He worked at the corporation until his death, providing his family with a secure income, but Ceannt found the drudgery of his working life as a clerk unfulfilling and he longed to be part of something more meaningful.

The first inklings of his later politicisation came with his involvement in the centenary celebrations of the 1798 rebellion and when he raised a flag in support of the Boers at the bottom of the garden at his home on Clonliffe Road. But the seeds of revolution were firmly sown when Ceannt joined the Gaelic League at a meeting of the Ard Craobh (Central Branch) in Dublin in 1899. He had shown a gift for languages from a young age: he learned French and German at school and was known to have visited Dublin's docks when foreign ships were in port, to converse with sailors in foreign languages. Although his study of the Irish language came later, he embraced it with enthusiasm, learning the language with the help of Fr Eugene O'Growney's *Easy Lessons in Irish* and some tutoring from his father. Within four years of joining the Gaelic League he was proficient enough in Irish to teach new members. Ceannt was a very active member of the Gaelic League, being a founder member of the Clontarf Branch in 1901 and a dedicated organiser of the annual Language Procession in Dublin city centre on St Patrick's Day. Significantly the Gaelic League brought Ceannt into contact with figures such as Patrick Pearse and Eoin MacNeill; according to his biographer, it was 'through this organisation that he developed a deeper devotion to Irish nationalism and made many friends who shared the same ideologies.'[2]

Ceannt was also a gifted musician. His brother Michael

recalled buying a cheap fiddle to practise on at home, which Éamonn borrowed and learned to play before Michael himself had a chance to get to grips with the instrument.[3] He first encountered the uilleann pipes through a colleague in Dublin Corporation, and this traditional instrument greatly appealed to Ceannt, who was becoming ever more involved in the Irish Ireland movement. He taught himself to play the pipes with the help of Martin Reilly, a blind piper whom he met on holidays in the West of Ireland.[4] In February 1900 Ceannt, along with Edward Martyn from Co. Galway, founded Cumann na bPíobairí (the Pipers' Association) as an independent offshoot of the Gaelic League, to promote and protect the tradition of uilleann pipe playing in Ireland. The Pipers' Association organised and paid for uilleann pipe players to travel to Dublin to play at *feiseanna*, playing a vital role in preserving a dying tradition.

Ceannt's talent as a piper eventually brought him to national attention in September 1908 when he travelled to Rome with members of the Catholic Young Men's Society (CYMS) who were participating in an athletics competition in honour of the jubilee of Pope Pius X. All the countries of Europe took part in the contest, with the exception of England and Russia, and the CYMS was anxious to assert the independent national identity of the Irish contingent. Ceannt, dressed in a distinctive red-and-green traditional costume, led the Irish contestants into the stadium with his pipe music. One of the Irish team described the reaction of the audience: 'Both the costume and musical instrument excited the attention of the enormous concourse present and achieved the object sought to be obtained vis., that Ireland was not England.'[5] Later, the Irish team was invited to an audience with Pope Pius X, at which Ceannt marched three times around the audience chamber playing 'O'Donnell Abú'. The Pope was said to have been very taken with his pipe playing and gave him a papal blessing at the end of his performance.

It was through the Gaelic League and the Pipers' Association that Ceannt met Frances O'Brennan (known as Áine), who was his pupil in the Gaelic League and held the position of honorary treasurer in the Pipers' Association. Áine was born in Dublin in September 1880. Her father, Frank, who died shortly after she was born, is believed to have been involved in the Fenian movement. She joined the Gaelic League after finishing school at Dominican College, Eccles Street. Éamonn and Áine were married in 1905 at St James's Church on James's Street, Dublin. The ceremony was conducted through Irish and the couple signed the marriage register using the Irish version of their names. In the symbolic exchanging of money, Éamonn insisted that French five-franc coins were used instead of English ones. Their son Rónán was born a year later, in June 1906, and the couple eventually moved to a house at 2 Dolphin Terrace, South Circular Road.

Although Ceannt's activities were mostly confined to cultural nationalism from 1900, after 1910 he became increasingly involved in political nationalism, the radicalisation of his views being concurrent with the reawakening of the Home Rule movement during this period. In 1911 Ceannt was a member of the United Societies Committee, which met at Sinn Féin headquarters on Harcourt Street. The committee was set up to protest against the impending visit of King George V to Ireland. In 1912 he attended a public meeting on Sackville Street in support of the Home Rule Bill, at which Patrick Pearse and Eoin MacNeill spoke. He increasingly came to the attention of advanced nationalists through his contributions to newspapers and journals, such as Pearse's Irish-language newspaper *An Barr Buadh*. Seán Mac Diarmada saw Ceannt's potential as a separatist revolutionary and swore him into the IRB in December 1912.

Ceannt's involvement with the Irish Volunteers began when Michael O'Rahilly invited him to attend a meeting at Wynn's Hotel on 11 November 1913, where it was decided to form the Irish Volunteers. Ceannt was also present at the subsequent meeting in the Rotunda Rink on 25 November, when the Irish Volunteers were founded. He was elected to the Provisional Committee of the Volunteers and he signed up to his local company – A Company, 4th Battalion, Dublin Brigade. The formation of a military organisation like the Volunteers suited Ceannt, who was 'by nature a physical force man'.[6] He was quickly promoted to captain of A Company and later appointed commandant of the 4th Battalion. At a meeting of the Provisional Committee on 16 June 1914 at which it was decided to allow John Redmond, leader of the Irish

Parliamentary Party, to nominate twenty-five representatives to the Provisional Committee, he was one of nine committee members who voted against the proposal.

Ceannt was present during the landing of arms for the Irish Volunteers at Howth on 26 July 1914. According to Áine Ceannt, while the Volunteers were returning to Dublin, Éamonn reacted to the bayoneting of his men by the British military by firing his Mauser gun and injuring Lance Corporal Finney in the ankle.[7] During the split in the Irish Volunteers regarding the participation of Irish men in the war in Europe, Éamonn Ceannt was a key organiser of a nationalist conference held in the library of the Gaelic League at Parnell Square on 9 September 1914. At this meeting it was decided to take advantage of the war by staging a rebellion against British rule in Ireland. Ceannt later told his wife, Áine: 'We Volunteers, an armed body, could not let this opportunity pass without striking a blow while England is at war. We would be a disgrace to our generation.'[8]

By mid-1915 Ceannt occupied key positions of influence in both the Irish Volunteers and the IRB. As well as being appointed commandant of the 4th Battalion, Dublin Brigade, he was also director of communications for the Irish Volunteers. In this capacity he created An Post Gaelach, a secure postal system for the organisation. In May 1915 Ceannt, along with Patrick Pearse and Joseph Plunkett, formed the Military Council of the IRB, and they were tasked by senior IRB figures with planning the rebellion. Meetings of the Military

Council were often held at Ceannt's home and later were also attended by Thomas Clarke and Seán Mac Diarmada. From January 1916 James Connolly was also present. At their secret meetings the date of the rebellion – Easter Sunday, 23 April – was eventually decided upon and battalion commandants were given their designated garrison areas. Éamonn Ceannt's 4th Battalion was assigned to the South Dublin Union, a large workhouse complex for Dublin's poor, destitute and mentally ill to the south-west of Dublin city centre, now St James's Hospital.

On Palm Sunday, 16 April 1916, Ceannt informed his wife that he was taking a week's holiday from his work in the corporation. He used this time to prepare for the Rising by attending meetings and carrying out reconnaissance work to prepare for the capture and defence of the South Dublin Union. Ceannt grew increasingly nervous of arrest by the authorities and from Tuesday onwards he slept with his gun next to his bed. On Holy Thursday the Ceannts' home was busy with the arrival of couriers, who received dispatches containing instructions for the Rising to be distributed around the country. On Good Friday Ceannt instructed his personal courier, J. J. Styles, to deliver ammunition to a grocer's shop located opposite the South Dublin Union. It was Holy Saturday before Ceannt informed his wife, Áine, that the Rising was due to take place the next day.

Ceannt was devastated to hear of Eoin MacNeill's counter-manding order later that evening. He went around Dublin city trying in vain to make contact with members of the Military Council before returning home at 5 a.m. He awoke later that morning to the news that the council was to meet that day to discuss alternative plans. At the meeting Ceannt supported the decision to rise on the following day, Easter Monday.

Ceannt left his home on the morning of Easter Monday and walked the short distance to Emerald Square, where the 4th Battalion was due to mobilise at 11 a.m. His wife, son and mother-in-law also left the house at Dolphin Terrace and went to Cathal Brugha's house at Fitzwilliam Terrace, where they stayed for the duration of the Rising. When he arrived at Emerald Square, Ceannt quickly realised that he was commanding a drastically reduced battalion: just 120 of the 700 members had turned out. These included Vice-Commandant Cathal Brugha and Lieutenant William Cosgrave, later first president of the Executive Council of the Irish Free State.

The South Dublin Union was a strategically vital position for the rebels during the Easter Rising. It was located in close proximity to British Army garrisons at Richmond Barracks (Inchicore), Islandbridge Barracks and the Royal Hospital Kilmainham. British troops arriving from the Curragh were likely to pass through Kingsbridge Station, also near Ceannt's position. The South Dublin Union was a vast area of command, encompassing over fifty acres, which included both areas of open field and building complexes separated by labyrinthine streets. For Ceannt to seize and defend such a sizeable area with just 120 Volunteers was a gargantuan task. Their numbers were further stretched by the need to allocate some Volunteers to command strategic outposts at Roe's Distillery in James's Street, Jameson's Distillery in Marrowbone Lane and Watkins' Brewery in Ardee Street. Less than half of those who turned out accompanied Ceannt to take the South Dublin Union itself. The presence of some 3,282 inmates as well as staff at the South Dublin Union posed a further challenge.

The 4th Battalion entered the South Dublin Union via the two main entrances to the complex. Ceannt took control of the Rialto entrance with ease and his small force set about fortifying the auxiliary workhouse located opposite the gate. A second party, under Brugha, seized the James's Street entrance. The nurses' home at this end of the complex was identified as a suitable headquarters and was barricaded by the Volunteers.

The South Dublin Union garrison began to make their presence felt when a small group of Volunteers opened fire on a company of British soldiers making their way to Dublin Castle. British troops responded quickly and an attack on the complex began at around 1 p.m., when Volunteer positions were hit by machine-gun fire coming from the Royal Hospital and troops launched an assault on the Rialto gate. There were heavy casualties on both sides during this fighting. The rebels lost control of the Rialto gate and were forced back to the Hospital 2–3 building at the centre of the complex. During the fighting here a nurse, Margaret Keogh, was accidentally shot dead by British troops. The fighting descended into a 'bloody game of hide and seek' between Volunteers and

British soldiers in the corridors, streets and open spaces of the South Dublin Union.[9] The majority of the rebels had retreated to headquarters at the nurses' home when firing eventually ceased by nightfall.

Throughout his command of the South Dublin Union, Ceannt was respected and admired by those who fought under him and he demonstrated inspirational leadership throughout Easter Week. One garrison member, James Coughlan, recorded that he felt confident of Ceannt's ability 'to lead us in whatever the future might hold'.[10] Every evening Ceannt gathered the Volunteers together and, following a recitation of the rosary and other prayers, he addressed the men and informed them of whatever developments had taken place that day. On Monday evening he read aloud the Proclamation and described how he was a signatory to the document. He told them of his expectations that Volunteers were rising around the country and that German help was on its way. On Tuesday he provided a morale boost for the Volunteers, stating that 'he was proud of his men, and thanked God for giving him the great pleasure of leading them'.[11]

Tuesday and Wednesday were relatively quiet days at the South Dublin Union, but the garrison sensed that an attack was imminent. A major British assault began on Thursday afternoon when troops entered the complex, advancing in waves and attacking with machine guns and grenades. Intense hand-to-hand fighting followed, during which Ceannt shot dead an RIC constable, Christopher Miller. Cathal Brugha was badly wounded by an exploding grenade thrown over a barricade in the nurses' home. Undaunted, he continued to fire at the barricade. Brugha's singing of 'God Save Ireland' caused Ceannt to rush to his side and they exchanged words in Irish, bringing Ceannt to tears. The rebels continued to fight on and the British troops eventually withdrew from Volunteer headquarters at the nurses' home. Firing ceased at 9.30 p.m. that evening and the British withdrew from the complex back to the Royal Hospital.

There were no further attacks on the South Dublin Union for the rest of the week. In his address to the Volunteers on Saturday evening, Ceannt anticipated another major assault by the British military. But on Sunday morning Thomas Mac-Donagh was seen walking towards the South Dublin Union with Fr Albert and Fr Aloysius under the cover of a white flag; he had already discussed the surrender of his garrison at Jacob's biscuit factory with Brigadier General Lowe. MacDonagh informed Ceannt of the order to surrender and Ceannt in turn relayed the information to his men. He told the garrison that they could continue the fight if they wished and that he would continue to lead them, but stated that if a man as dedicated to the cause of Irish freedom as Tom Clarke had surrendered, then the 4th Battalion could honourably do so.[12] The men agreed to surrender.

The injured – including Cathal Brugha, who had twenty-five wounds to his body – were removed to hospital and the remaining men prepared for the march to the surrender point at St Patrick's Park. A British officer present expressed his surprise to Ceannt at the size of the garrison; given the fierceness of the engagements during the week, he had expected a much bigger number than the forty-one men he encountered that Sunday at the South Dublin Union.

Having disarmed at St Patrick's Park, the 4th Battalion marched with the garrison of Jacob's biscuit factory to Richmond Barracks. They were held there overnight in cramped conditions and the following morning Ceannt was identified in the gymnasium as one of the leaders of the rebellion to be court-martialled. His field-general court martial began on 3 May, with General Blackader presiding. The prosecution called just one witness, Major J. A. Armstrong, while Ceannt called four witnesses in his defence: Thomas MacDonagh, John MacBride, Richard Davys and Patrick Sweeney. Unknown to Ceannt, MacDonagh had been executed at dawn that morning. In his evidence, Armstrong incorrectly linked Ceannt to the garrison from Jacob's biscuit factory present at St Patrick's Park on Sunday 30 April, and he also stated that Ceannt's name was at the top of a list of names of armed men who surrendered there.[13] Ceannt cross-examined Armstrong, and MacBride then testified for the defence that Ceannt was not a member of the Jacob's biscuit factory garrison. His two other witnesses gave similar evidence when the trial resumed the next day, but to no avail. Ceannt was found guilty of participating in the rebellion and was sentenced to execution by firing squad. General Maxwell confirmed the death sentence on 6 May.

Áine Ceannt knew little of her husband's whereabouts once he left their home on Easter Monday for the South Dublin Union. Following the surrender she was fraught with worry and desperate for any information on what had happened, and what might happen, to her husband. She and Éamonn's brother Michael found some consolation in a newspaper report claiming that Éamonn was to be sentenced to three years' penal servitude. With the assistance of Johnny Foley, a family friend who had been secretary to the lord mayor of Dublin, Áine gained admission to Kilmainham Gaol, to which Ceannt had been transferred from Richmond Barracks, on Saturday morning, 6 May. On entering her husband's cell, she observed 'that his Sam Brown [*sic*] belt was gone, and that his uniform was slightly torn'.[14] At this juncture Áine still held out hope that the death sentence would be reprieved, but Ceannt was informed at some point on Saturday or Sunday that his execution would be carried out on the morning of 8 May. He began writing his last letters to loved ones and a statement regarding the Easter Rising, in which he criticised the 'grave disaster' caused by the surrender of the rebels and advised future generations to 'fight to the finish'. He wrote that he bore 'no ill will' to those he fought against. He praised the garrison of the South Dublin Union:

I wish to record the magnificent gallantry and fearless, calm determination of the men who fought with me. All, all, were simply splendid. Even I knew no fear nor panic and shrunk from no risk even as I shrink not now from the death which faces me at daybreak.[15]

At 10 p.m. on Sunday evening a soldier knocked on the door of the home of Nell Ceannt, where Áine was staying that evening. He told her that her husband wished to see her at Kilmainham Gaol. Ceannt's brothers Michael and Richard were already in the car. During the visit Ceannt indicated his hope that he might yet be given a reprieve, as it had been some days since any executions had taken place. He gave Áine a letter for their son Rónán, asking her to tell him that he had died for Ireland. As Richard Ceannt left the prison a soldier, the commandant of the prison, informed him that the death sentence would be carried out.

Éamonn Ceannt was attended to by Fr Augustine during his final hours and wrote his final letter to Áine at 2.30 a.m. on 8 May 1916, just over one hour before he faced the firing squad. She learned of his death later that morning when she visited Fr Augustine at the Capuchin Friary on Church Street.

CON COLBERT

Con Colbert was just twenty-five years old at Easter 1916, making him the youngest of the leaders of the Easter Rising to be executed. Known to his family as Cornelius, he was born in Monalena, Co. Limerick. His father, Michael, was a small farmer and the family soon moved to a farm called Galeview near Athea, Co. Limerick. One of his uncles is believed to have participated in the Fenian Rising of 1867. Colbert was the fourth youngest of thirteen children and his mother, Nora (née MacDermott), died aged thirty-seven, when he was still a young boy. The census returns for 1901 show Colbert, aged eleven, living at the Galeview farm with his widowed father and five siblings. To alleviate the financial pressures on his father, who was raising a large family alone, Con moved to Dublin, where he stayed with his sister Catherine at 7 Clifton Terrace, Ranelagh Road. He attended the O'Connell school on North Richmond Street for a brief period, where, like others of his generation, the Christian Brothers instilled in him a knowledge of the past glories and failures of Irish nationalism. He found employment at Kennedy's Bakery on Parnell Street where he worked until his death; in the 1911 census he listed his occupation as 'bookkeeper (bakery)'.[1]

Colbert was an early member of the nationalist youth organisation Na Fianna Éireann. Founded in August 1909 at Camden Hall by Bulmer Hobson and Constance Markievicz, Na Fianna Éireann was the nationalist alternative to other uniformed organisations for boys, including Robert Baden-Powell's Boy Scouts, which was seen as having a British imperialist outlook. Like other scouting organisations, Fianna members learned skills such as Morse signalling, camp life, map reading, first aid and swimming; they also participated in drilling exercises and carried out rifle practice. What made Na Fianna Éireann unique was the emphasis placed on Irish language, folklore, history and culture. The name of the organisation was inspired by the mythological band of warriors, the Fianna, who followed the hero of Gaelic Ireland, Fionn Mac Cumhaill. Na Fianna Éireann also offered classes in the Irish language, which Colbert learned to speak fluently. Again in the 1911 census he records that he was proficient in both Irish and English.

From its inception Na Fianna Éireann became the focus of Colbert's young life. His friend in Limerick, Madge Daly (sister of Edward Daly), later recalled:

He gave [Na Fianna Éireann] every moment of his spare time, and even during his summer holidays he would don his Fianna uniform and cycle from place to place getting a few boys together to start a new sluagh. With his earnestness and enthusiasm he proved a most successful recruiting agent.[2]

Colbert commanded the Inchicore *sluagh* of Na Fianna Éireann and through his prominence in the organisation he became chief scout of Ireland. He brought the Fianna boys on camping trips, studied military manuals and trained Fianna instructors in how to teach drill. Hobson, a founder member of Na Fianna Éireann, was also a key figure in the IRB and used his influence in the Fianna to recruit new members to the secret organisation. Colbert was one of the first to be sworn in to a circle of IRB members within the Fianna known as the John Mitchel Literary and Debating Society. Other members of this circle included Seán McGarry, Liam Mellows, Pádraig Ó Riain and Seán Heuston. By December 1912 Colbert himself was swearing in members: Garry Holohan recalled Colbert administering the Fenian oath to him at the Fianna offices on D'Olier Street that month.[3]

Colbert's work with the Fianna brought him into contact with Patrick Pearse in the autumn of 1910 and Pearse offered him the position of part-time drill instructor at St Enda's. When Pearse suggested that he pay Colbert a small fee for his efforts, Colbert was so horrified at the prospect of being paid for national work 'that Pearse had to apologise and drop the idea'.[4] Like his other activities with the Fianna, Colbert took his role as drill instructor at St Enda's very seriously. Desmond Ryan, a pupil at the school, recalled one evening session when Colbert had an 'outburst' over the lack of enthusiasm of some of the boys in the class. He warned them that although they did not realise it now, the 'drills and fencings and marchings' he was instructing them in would someday be useful to them if they wanted to remain living in Ireland.[5]

Unbeknownst to Pearse, Colbert recruited some of the older university students lodging at St Enda's into the IRB, including Desmond Ryan, Éamonn Bulfin, Frank Burke and Joseph Sweeney. At this point Pearse had not yet been sworn into the IRB.

Con Colbert was a dedicated, serious and hard-working person, devoted to both his Catholicism and his desire for an independent Gaelic Ireland. His sister Elizabeth was surprised to discover shortly after his death that he had been writing love letters to a Dublin girl called Lucy Smith. Elizabeth had thought that he was so serious about his nationalist activities that he had no time for romantic interests.[6] According to Colbert's IRB colleague Holohan, 'his soul burned for everything Gaelic and Irish'.[7] As well as learning to speak Irish fluently, he also wore clothes only of Irish manufacture. A teetotaller, Colbert was a devout Catholic who attended Mass daily. Kathleen Clarke, the wife of Tom Clarke, recalled Colbert's objections to her holding a *céilidhe* on Palm Sunday 1916, a week before the Rising, as a cover for an IRB meeting:

Con Colbert came into the shop to protest against a céilidhe being held in Lent. He was deeply religious, and did not think it right. I could not explain the reason for it to him, so I told him not to be so squeamish and to dance while he could, as he might be dancing at the end of a rope one of these days. I fear I shocked him, and I was sorry the minute the words were out of my mouth. I was sorry for having being so flippant, but I was under great strain at the time.[8]

The earnestness with which Colbert went about his work for the nationalist movement may have contributed to his disillusionment in the aftermath of the Rising, when he discovered that the people of Ireland were not as devoted to the cause of an independent Ireland as he was.

On the foundation of the Irish Volunteers in November

1913, Colbert was a member of the Provisional Committee. He was later made captain of F Company, 4th Battalion of the Dublin Brigade Irish Volunteers, based in Inchicore, where he also commanded a *sluagh* of Na Fianna Éireann boys. Inchicore and its surrounds was a difficult area in which to recruit and train the Irish Volunteers, as the presence of a British Army garrison at Richmond Barracks meant that a large section of the population did not sympathise with Irish nationalism. The company initially attracted 800 members, but following the split in the Volunteers in September 1914, just forty or fifty of the original group turned up for drill practice at the Workman's Club in Inchicore, with the other Redmondite Volunteers training at the courthouse in Kilmainham.[9]

In the weeks leading up to the Rising Colbert acted as personal bodyguard to Patrick Pearse, which placed him close to the key figures organising the rebellion, although it is uncertain when he was made aware of the date of the Rising and the details of the plan. Madge Daly recalled meeting him in Dublin the week before the Rising and although they did not discuss the rebellion openly, she 'knew instinctively that Con was aware of the coming test and we both felt that it might be our last meeting'.[10]

During Holy Week Colbert was involved in the movement of arms and ammunition around Dublin. He left his sister's house in Ranelagh to stay closer to his company at the home of the Cooney family, 16 Upper Basin Street, where he spent the nights before the rebellion. On Holy Thursday he held a meeting of F Company at Dolphin's Barn next to the Grand Canal. Robert Holland, a member of the company, observed that 'there were more men there than usual' and that some new recruits were in attendance.[11] On Good Friday Colbert called to Holland's house to tell him to be ready for mobilisation and to ask him to warn the other men to bring with them the tools of their trade, as he anticipated street-fighting would take place.

Colbert returned at 6 a.m. on Easter Sunday morning to tell Holland that the Rising was off. The next morning Colbert was woken at the Cooney house at 7 a.m. by Seán O'Brien, a member of C Company, 4th Battalion, who told him the Rising was to begin that day. Colbert got up from his bed, put on a navy suit and headed for Mass, dropping off mobilisation orders on his way home.[12] On his return the Cooney sisters helped Colbert and his lieutenant, Christopher Byrne, to get ready and pack their haversacks. Annie Cooney-O'Brien remembered:

> During the time I was buckling him up Con – who had not a note in his head – was singing 'For Tone is coming back again' he was so excited and charmed that at last the fight was coming off. He thought of nothing else. The pair went off, wheeling their bicycles which were loaded up with pikes, their rifles and small arms. We saw them off at the door and waited till they were out of sight.[13]

The men were headed for Emerald Square, for the mobilisation of the 4th Battalion at 11 a.m.

Colbert received his orders, from Battalion Commandant Éamonn Ceannt, to seize control of Watkins' Brewery, Ardee Street. The majority of the 4th Battalion were to seize and defend the South Dublin Union, but Watkins' Brewery was one of three strategic outposts, the others being Roe's Distillery, Mount Brown and Jameson's Distillery, Marrowbone Lane. Watkins' Brewery was located in the Coombe, and Colbert's task was to halt the approach of British troops from the south-west.

Colbert and his much depleted company of just fifteen men seized control of the brewery without any difficulty. They erected barricades but were undisturbed and did not even see any British military during their time there. Frustrated by the lack of action at his outpost, on Tuesday morning Colbert sent a dispatch to the GPO outlining his position. He received a reply from James Connolly, instructing him to transfer his men to Marrowbone Lane to reinforce the fifty Irish Volunteers and twenty members of Cumann na mBan already there.

When Colbert's company arrived at Marrowbone Lane on Tuesday, the men and women there were recovering from a fierce attack that afternoon, during which they had repelled an attempt by the British military to take control of the building. Colbert took over from Captain Seamus Murphy to command the garrison. From Wednesday to Friday the rebels had to contend with sniper fire, but they held their position and suffered no casualties. Colbert's military strategy was admired by the Volunteers, in particular his decision to place a sniper in an open position close to the canal, allowing the Volunteers to prevent the entry of British soldiers into the South Dublin Union via a back entrance.

By Sunday morning British sniper fire had ceased and the strength of the garrison's position led them to believe that the rebellion had been a success. It came as a great surprise, therefore, when Thomas MacDonagh arrived late on Sunday afternoon to inform Colbert and Murphy of the order to surrender. At 6.30 p.m. Ceannt and the Volunteers from the South Dublin Union arrived at Marrowbone Lane. Robert Holland described the scene:

> Commandant Ceannt, a British Amy officer and a clergyman, who was either a Carmelite or a Franciscan, entered the front gate. Ceannt shook hands with Colbert, Murphy and Murray and the six of them had a conversation lasting only a few moments. Colbert saluted Ceannt and walked back towards me in the yard. I asked him what was the news and he said that all was over. When I heard this I felt kind of sick in my stomach, putting it mildly, and everybody else felt the same, I'm sure. It came as a great shock. Colbert could hardly speak as he stood in the yard for a moment or two. He was completely stunned.[14]

Already disillusioned by the failure of many of his Fianna and Volunteer men to turn out on Easter Monday, Colbert was sent into further despair by his realisation that the people of Ireland had not joined the Volunteers in their rebellion. Following the surrender the men were brought to Richmond Barracks and suffered jeering from people gathered along the route. Colbert was heard to say that he would rather be executed than imprisoned, as life would be torture living among people who had shown such contempt for their efforts to free Ireland.[15]

Colbert was court-martialled on 4 May 1916. In his evidence the prosecution witness, Major J. A. Armstrong, incorrectly placed Colbert with the garrison at Jacob's biscuit factory on Easter Sunday. Colbert, however, chose not to cross-examine him, called no witnesses in his defence and made no statement countering Armstrong's evidence. Colbert was transferred to Kilmainham Gaol and his death sentence was confirmed on Sunday 7 May. Annie Cooney, who had also been imprisoned in Kilmainham, saw Colbert at Mass in the prison that morning and he waved to her as if to say farewell.[16]

Before his execution Colbert asked to see the wife of Seamus Murphy from the Marrowbone Lane garrison; she was also being held in the gaol. Colbert told her that he was proud to die for Irish independence and that he considered himself 'one of the lucky ones'.[17] He spent his final hours writing letters to his family members, including one to his sister Lila, in which he explained that he did not send for her as a visit 'would grieve us both too much'.[18]

Con Colbert was attended by Fr Augustine as he faced

the firing squad at dawn on 8 May 1916 and the volleys were heard by the Cumann na mBan women of Marrowbone Lane, from inside the prison.

THOMAS KENT

Thomas Kent, one of only two men connected to the Rising who were executed outside Dublin, was born on 29 August 1865 at Bawnard House, Castlelyons, near the town of Fermoy, Co. Cork. Bawnard House was part of the large farm of 200 acres owned by his father, David Kent. His mother, Mary (née Rice), was from the local area; one of her brothers was a priest in the nearby town of Mitchelstown and another brother was coroner of Fermoy. Mary gave birth to nine children, of whom six survived to adulthood.[1] Thomas and his four brothers – Edmond, David, William and Richard – were living at Bawnard House at the time of the Easter Rising in 1916. His sister Lizzie had left the family home at this point.

Following his father's death in the mid-1880s, Thomas had moved to America and settled in Boston. There he secured employment at the office of an old family friend, Thomas B. Noonan, 'Catholic publisher and church-furnisher'.[2] While in America he learned to speak the Irish language and became manager of the journal of the Philo-Celtic society.

Meanwhile back in Ireland, Thomas's brothers were active in the Land League movement that was sweeping the country. The impact of the Land League campaign was felt strongly in north Co. Cork. In 1887 a riot occurred in the nearby town of Mitchelstown during the trial of Land League campaigner William O'Brien and Tipperary farmer John Mandeville. Police opened fire on the crowd, shooting dead three people in an incident that became known as the Mitchelstown Massacre. In 1889 William, Edmond, David and Richard were arrested along with a local priest, Fr O'Dwyer, for their involvement in a Land League effort to stop the payment of rents by tenants to landlords. Richard avoided imprisonment on account of his youth. The others were convicted and served their sentences in Cork Gaol, where they carried out hard labour.

Thomas returned to Ireland and soon he too became caught up in the land agitation movement in Cork. He served a term of imprisonment for his activities along with his brother William. On their release from prison, William described how he and Thomas 'were met by thousands of people in Fermoy who escorted us all the way home to Bawnard'.[3]

With the collapse of the Land League and Home Rule movements following the split over Charles Stewart Parnell's association with the O'Shea divorce case in 1890, Thomas Kent withdrew from his involvement in politics. Kent's nationalist activities were now confined to his local branch of the Gaelic League, where he ran Irish, music and dancing classes. He was later described by Liam de Róiste, a Cork activist in the Gaelic League and Irish Volunteers, as 'a straight, strong countryman, who was outspoken'.[4] Kent abstained from drinking alcohol and he was unmarried at the time of his death in 1916.

Following the formation of the Irish Volunteers in Dublin in November 1913, Kent's enthusiasm for the Irish nationalist movement was reawakened. Thomas, along with his brother David, was involved in organising the Irish Volunteers in North Cork. The Clonmult Corps of the Irish Volunteers, of which Thomas was a leading member, was said to be 'the first teetotal company in Ireland'.[5] In late 1914 or early 1915 Thomas and David organised a group of hurlers from Clonmult to march to the village of Dungourney to disrupt a British Army recruitment meeting. They addressed the crowd, 'advising them to join the Volunteers and have nothing whatever to do with the British Army'.[6] After the split in the Volunteers Kent no longer associated with the Clonmult Corps but continued to be actively involved with Irish Volunteer activities in the county. In October 1915 he represented his district at the Irish Volunteers convention at the Abbey Theatre.

In January 1916 Kent was arrested along with Terence MacSwiney at Ballynoe, Conna, Co. Cork, where the pair were addressing a Volunteer recruitment meeting. At their subsequent trial Kent was charged with possession of a revolver and ammunition at the meeting and for being heard to say to the crowd that it would be better to 'die in Ireland and be buried here than be thrown into a hole in Flanders'.[7] Kent and MacSwiney were acquitted, but shortly afterwards Kent received a two-month sentence for possession of arms found at the family home.

There was almost no rebel activity in Cork during the Easter Rising in 1916. The planned landing of an arms shipment in Co. Kerry was to be the catalyst for a rising in Cork. When the *Aud* was scuppered on Good Friday, plans for a rebellion were thrown into disarray. Although the Cork Volunteers did mobilise under Tomás MacCurtain and Terence MacSwiney on Easter Sunday, confusion caused by MacNeill's counter-manding order prevented a rebellion from taking place. For the duration of the Rising in Dublin, the Kent brothers feared arrest and did not sleep in the family home at Bawnard.

With the surrender of the rebels in Dublin, the Kents considered it safe to return home. However, at about 4.30 a.m. on the morning of 2 May, a party of RIC men arrived at Bawnard. According to Frank King, an RIC constable stationed at

Fermoy, they had received orders 'to arrest all the prominent "Sinn Féiners" in the district'.[8] Accounts differ as to the response of the Kents to the arrival of the RIC at their home. William Kent described how he stuck his head out of a window on the eastern side of the house and called out 'Who's there?' The police announced their presence and he went to Thomas, who was sleeping on the other side of the house, telling him: 'The whole place is surrounded. We are caught like rats in a trap.' The police then informed the brothers of their intention to arrest the whole family. William stated that the family's response was to declare: 'We are soldiers of the Irish Republic, and there is no surrender.'[9] According to Frank King, however, the brothers were heard telling Head Constable Rowe: 'We will not surrender until we leave some of you dead.'[10]

The Kents were armed with three shotguns and one rifle. Their mother, Mary, by now in her eighties, was also in the house. Again, accounts differ as to which party fired the first shot, but a fierce shootout ensued. As the RIC began to retreat from the house a number of shots were fired, fatally wounding Constable Rowe. David Kent was seriously wounded, losing two of his fingers and receiving a deep wound in his side. Shots continued to be exchanged for the next couple of hours until military reinforcements arrived and the Kents surrendered. William assessed the damage done and described how he believed a statue of Our Lady prevented further casualties in the household:

The house was wrecked. Not a pane of glass was left unbroken. The interior was tattooed with marks of rifle bullets. The altar and statues in the Oratory alone escaped destruction. All around the altar plaster was knocked off the walls but not one of the statues was struck. At one time the fire of the attackers was attracted to the window of the Oratory where they thought a girl was firing at them. Strange to say, it was the statue of our Lady of Lourdes they saw from the outside. The same statue was bought by my brother Tom at the sale of Father Ferris's household effects. Father Ferris had brought it from Lourdes and I attribute to it the fact that our lives and home were saved from complete destruction.[11]

The Kent brothers emerged from the window of the house to make their surrender. William and Thomas were handcuffed but Richard was not. He tried to escape by bounding over a nearby hedge but was shot during the attempt. The rest of the family were lined up outside the house, and, according to William, it was suggested that they would be shot straight away. However, a soldier intervened and took the four brothers and their mother under military escort to the military barracks at Fermoy.

The injured brothers, David and Richard, were taken to Fermoy Military Hospital. Richard died from his wounds two days later. William Kent later credited Dr Brody at the hospital with saving David's life, as he refused to allow him to face his court martial until he recovered from his wounds. It was two weeks before David was transferred to Cork Detention Barracks and by that time public opinion had turned against the executions of the rebels. David was eventually court-martialled at Richmond Barracks on 14 June, when he was found guilty and sentenced to death. His death sentence was commuted to life imprisonment and he was held in Dartmoor and Pentonville prisons in England. He was released as part of the general amnesty of prisoners in 1917 and was subsequently elected three times as a Sinn Féin representative for the constituency of East Cork.

His brother Thomas was not so fortunate. He and William were court-martialled almost immediately, on 4 May 1916. Frank King gave evidence at William's trial, stating that he was 'a quiet, inoffensive type who had no "Sinn Féin" activities'.[12] William was acquitted as a result. Thomas was charged with the same offence as the leaders of the Easter Rising in Dublin – that he 'did an act to wit take part in an armed rebellion and in the waging of war against His Majesty the King'. Kent pleaded not guilty and stated to the court that during the siege he had 'never fired, or had arms in my hand'.[13] There were five prosecution witnesses: three RIC members and two members of the British military. Thomas Kent was sentenced to death by firing squad and this was confirmed by Maxwell on 6 May. He was executed in the early hours of 9 May at the detention barracks in Cork. His last request was that no Irishman would be part of the firing squad, and the execution was carried out by soldiers from the Scottish Borderers. His body was buried in the grounds of the barracks.

SEÁN MAC DIARMADA

Seán Mac Diarmada was born John Joseph McDermott in January 1883. The McDermotts lived in the townland of Laghty Barr, Co. Leitrim, near the village of Kiltyclogher, in the north-east of the county. His father, Donald, was a carpenter by trade and his mother, Mary (née McMurrow), was also from the local area. Mac Diarmada was the third youngest of ten children. Although his childhood was mostly a happy one, tragedy struck with the death of his mother when Mac Diarmada was just nine years old. He attended Corracloona National School where he was considered 'above average in terms of local academic ability', although he struggled with mathematics.[1] In 1902 and again in 1903 he studied for the King's Scholarship Examination to be accepted to train as a national schoolteacher. In spite of tuition from a local master, James Gilmartin, Mac Diarmada failed to gain a place on two occasions owing to his weakness in maths.

His school friends from his teenage years remembered Mac Diarmada 'as one of the school's best pupils, bright in every sense of the word, lively and fond of boyhood games, good-natured and even-tempered, one who excelled at penmanship', and his teacher, Master P. McGauran, recalled Mac Diarmada as 'a dark-haired comely boy with smiling face and dark-blue eyes'.[2] McGauran taught him Irish and book-keeping at night school following his failed attempts to become a national schoolteacher. It was McGauran who nurtured his love of Irish history. Mac Diarmada became interested in rebel stories when his sister Katie gave him a copy of Abbé MacGeoghegan's *History of Ireland* when he was fourteen years old. McGauran developed this interest, introducing Mac Diarmada to nationalist texts including A. M. Sullivan's *History of Ireland* and *Speeches from the Dock*. McGauran remembered that Mac Diarmada was not a bookworm in general, but that 'books relating to Ireland, her language, her heroes, or her history were welcome to him'.[3]

Local and national events at the turn of the century also helped to foster his growing sense of nationalism. The commemoration of the 1798 rebellion, protests against the Boer War, the spread of the GAA and the evictions of local families living on the estate of Lord Tottenham all had an impact on shaping the political views of the young Mac Diarmada.

There were few opportunities in Co. Leitrim in the early 1900s for a young man like Mac Diarmada to earn a living. In 1905 he moved to Belfast, where he found employment as a conductor on the Belfast trams. In this northern city Mac Diarmada found himself in the midst of a hotbed of republican activity. Around this time the IRB had begun to reorganise itself and Belfast was at the centre of this reawakening. Denis McCullough and Bulmer Hobson were the driving forces and they rid the Belfast IRB of its older membership and established the Dungannon Clubs, which promoted advanced nationalist ideas, including the withdrawal of Irish MPs from the Westminster parliament and the promotion of Irish industry. Mac Diarmada joined the Dungannon Clubs and was sworn into the Belfast IRB by McCullough. Soon he was addressing public meetings to recruit new members for the Dungannon Clubs. At first Mac Diarmada found it difficult on the speaking circuit as he was often jeered at by crowds, and on one occasion he lost his temper with a particularly hostile group of factory girls. Hobson noted, however, that 'after a little practice' Mac Diarmada became 'a fairly good speaker'.[4] When he lost his job on the trams he was given a position as a paid organiser for the Dungannon Clubs in Tyrone.

National politics brought Mac Diarmada home to Co. Leitrim in the summer of 1907, where a by-election campaign was taking place. Charles Dolan, an MP for the Irish Parliamentary Party in Westminster, had switched allegiances from the pro-Home Rule party to Sinn Féin and was persuaded to resign his seat and seek re-election as a Sinn Féin candidate. The Dungannon Clubs had been absorbed into the Sinn Féin organisation and Mac Diarmada, as a local man, was the ideal person to take charge of Dolan's campaign. It was a difficult canvass and Dolan was heavily defeated by the Irish Parliamentary Party candidate. However, Mac Diarmada's involvement in the campaign raised his profile as a national organiser.

Perhaps the most significant event in Mac Diarmada's political development was the return to Ireland of Tom Clarke in 1908. When Mac Diarmada went to Dublin after the North Leitrim election, he struck up a friendship with Clarke, who saw in him the youthful energy and enthusiasm that was needed to reinvigorate the IRB and prepare it for revolution. The partnership of Clarke and Mac Diarmada was instrumental in directing the course of events over the following eight years. Clarke's wife, Kathleen, recalled the closeness of their relationship:

[Mac Diarmada] became Tom's loyal and loved comrade. He

did all his organising under Tom's guidance; Tom being older and more experienced, he trusted him completely. Indeed, they trusted each other completely.[5]

Mac Diarmada settled in Dublin and followed Clarke's strategy of joining organisations such as the Gaelic League and the GAA, which allowed the IRB to maintain a presence in nationalist groups, something that would prove useful later on.

Mac Diarmada travelled throughout Ireland and Britain openly recruiting for Sinn Féin and secretly swearing in new members to the IRB. According to Denis McCullough, it was Mac Diarmada's 'energy and organising ability' that was a significant factor 'in creating a group and guiding events to make the Rising possible'.[6] One of his achievements was Aonach na Nollaig, an annual showcase of Irish-produced goods held at the Rotunda, Dublin, in December. Mac Diarmada organised the event for Sinn Féin and it was deemed a great success because of the variety of goods on display. The Aonach facilitated the new trend for buying Christmas cards by providing a selection of Irish-made greetings cards, and at one Aonach there was even an aeroplane hanging in the hall.

From November 1910 Mac Diarmada was manager of the *Irish Freedom* newspaper, working from offices at 6 Findlater Place. The newspaper was set up on the initiative of Clarke as a mouthpiece for the IRB. Seán Prendergast, a regular reader, described the typical content of *Irish Freedom*:

It preached Republicanism, the Republicanism of Tone and Emmet – the doctrines of the men of '98, '48 and '67, the doctrine that the only cure for Irish ills, the undoing of the conquest of Ireland by England was by recourse to the policy of Separatism and armed revolt.[7]

His work with *Irish Freedom* meant that Mac Diarmada spent less time travelling around the country, but in 1911 he was out on the speaking platforms again, protesting against the visit of King George V.

In autumn 1911 Mac Diarmada fell ill with polio. He spent several months receiving treatment in the Mater Hospital, but the illness left him with a permanent lameness in his right leg. After leaving hospital, Mac Diarmada spent time convalescing in the homes of friends, including Tom Clarke's in-laws, the Daly family in Limerick. Madge Daly recalled seeing Mac Diarmada for the first time since his illness:

I will never forget the shock I got when I met him at the station. A few months before he was a joyous, buoyant lad, full of life and vigour. Then he looked a delicate, bearded, middle-aged man, only able to walk with a crutch and a stick.[8]

Although his illness forced Mac Diarmada to withdraw from political activities for much of 1911 and 1912, it did not dampen his spirit, and he returned to his work for the nationalist movement with renewed enthusiasm.

By early 1912 Clarke's manoeuvrings had succeeded in ousting the older generation of the IRB. In October 1912 Mac Diarmada travelled to America to attend a Clan na Gael conference in New Jersey. The trip was highly secretive but it brought him into contact with Irish-American organisations that could help with financing and organising a rebellion in Ireland.

Mac Diarmada's growing influence in the republican movement was brought to bear during the formation of the Irish Volunteers in 1913. He attended the meeting in Wynn's Hotel at which the creation of the organisation was proposed, and addressed an overflowing crowd in the concert hall at the Rotunda Rink when the Irish Volunteers were established on 25 November 1913. He became a member of the Provisional Committee of the organisation. Like Clarke, he felt betrayed by Bulmer Hobson's decision to support the inclusion of John Redmond's nominees on a new Provisional Committee in June 1914. Hobson resigned his position as editor of *Irish Freedom* and his relations with Mac Diarmada were very strained thereafter.

On 26 August 1914, the day of the gun-running, Clarke and Mac Diarmada spent much of the day travelling in a taxi to and from Howth, collecting the weapons landed by the Irish Volunteers at Howth harbour and bringing them to Dublin.

Mac Diarmada was arrested at Tuam, Co. Galway, on 18 May 1915 under the provisions of the Defence of the Realm Act. Accompanied by Liam Mellows, Mac Diarmada had been addressing a crowd that had gathered in the town square after attending Sunday Mass. When he uttered the phrase 'England's difficulty is Ireland's opportunity', an RIC detective and sergeant mounted the platform and arrested him.[9] Mac Diarmada managed to pass a weapon he was carrying in his pocket to another IRB man on the platform. During a brief conversation with Mellows to the side of the platform, Mac Diarmada secretly passed to him a notebook containing a list of IRB centres in the west. Mac Diarmada was transferred to Dublin, where he was held in Arbour Hill detention barracks and Beggars Bush Barracks while awaiting trial. He was tried on 9 June and sentenced to four months' imprisonment with hard labour. His incarceration in Mountjoy Prison meant that he missed out on important events in 1915, including the O'Donovan Rossa funeral and the suppression of the *Irish Freedom* newspaper. He was unaware of these happenings until his release from prison in September.

By late 1915 Mac Diarmada and Clarke held the respective positions of secretary and treasurer of the Supreme Council of the IRB, placing them in key positions of influence, and they ensured that Denis McCullough, who lived in Belfast and was too far away to control events in Dublin, was elected president. Mac Diarmada also became a member of the Military Council, joining Patrick Pearse, Joseph Plunkett and Éamonn Ceannt in formulating detailed plans for the Rising. Along with Clarke, Mac Diarmada worked largely in the background. In the months before the Rising Mac Diarmada made fewer public speeches, avoided bringing attention to himself and did not disclose details of the Rising to anyone unless it was absolutely necessary. Éamonn Dore later recalled the quiet dedication with which Mac Diarmada and Clarke carried out their work:

> They were so imbued with the ideal of freedom that they never cared who got the honours. On one occasion, when a member showed jealousy, Mac Diarmada turned to him and said 'S— does it matter who gets the credit as long as the job is done to our liking'.[10]

Mac Diarmada's manoeuvrings included confronting James Connolly in January 1916 over the possibility of an ICA rebellion and persuading him to hold off until a joint rising could take place with the Irish Volunteers. He travelled to England to meet with contacts, and from early 1916 he encouraged IRB men in Scotland and England to return to Ireland and organised for them to stay with the Plunketts at Larkfield House. In the month before the Rising he was involved in devising a plan to seize telegraph equipment from a wireless station at Cahirciveen, Co. Kerry, to communicate with the *Aud* arms ship coming from Germany. He decided to set up a wireless station in the house of his friend Dr Catherine Quinlan in Tralee for that purpose. According to Quinlan, 'this arrangement fell through' as a result of confusion over the timing of the arrival of the *Aud*.[11] Tragically it was also the case that three Irish Volunteers, who were part of a group travelling to Kerry from Dublin to carry out the seizure of equipment, drowned when their car drove off the pier at Ballykissane on Good Friday, 21 April 1916.

During the week before the Easter Rising, Mac Diarmada was mainly occupied with trying to prevent Eoin MacNeill from cancelling plans for the rebellion. At 8 a.m. on Good Friday he arrived at MacNeill's house with Thomas Mac-Donagh and Pearse to inform him that a shipment of arms was due to land in Co. Kerry. This news convinced MacNeill that a successful rising was possible and he agreed to allow the rebellion to go ahead. But news of the capture of Roger Casement and the sinking of the *Aud* persuaded him other-wise and on Holy Saturday MacNeill issued a countermand-ing order calling off Volunteer manoeuvres on Easter Sunday. Fionán Lynch recalled showing Mac Diarmada the counter-manding notice in the *Sunday Independent* after early Mass on Easter Sunday. He observed that 'it was the first and only time that I saw Seán really angry and upset'.[12] At a meeting of the Supreme Council at Liberty Hall later that day, Mac Diarmada was the driving force behind the decision to postpone the Rising until Easter Monday. Clarke was alone among the members of the Supreme Council in wanting the Rising to proceed that day. But Mac Diarmada, who was fully aware of military preparations for the rebellion, succeeded in persuading the council members of the need to postpone. Fearing arrest, he spent the night before the rebellion at Fleming's Hotel on Gardiner Place.

At noon on Easter Monday Mac Diarmada, wearing civilian clothes, travelled with Clarke by car to the GPO, his weak leg preventing him from marching with the others. His exact military rank in the GPO is uncertain, but he appears to have worked closely with Connolly, commander of the rebels in Dublin, and may have been his adjutant. It has been noted of Mac Diarmada that he was 'not a military man'. Although he was a member of B Company, 1st Battalion of the Irish Volunteers, his disability prevented him from participating in drill practice before the rebellion. Some of his duties included running the field hospital in the GPO, discouraging looters from stealing goods and sending out dispatches.

It was towards the end of the week, when Connolly was seriously wounded, Pearse exhausted and Plunkett seriously ill, that Mac Diarmada and Clarke increasingly took charge of military decisions in the GPO. Their authority 'was accepted without question by the garrison' and, along with The O'Rahilly, they gave orders to the men.[13] On Friday morning Mac Diarmada sensed the inevitability of the evacuation of the GPO. At dawn he gave instructions for outposts at Henry Street and Middle Abbey Street to withdraw and he instructed that the wounded rebels be removed to Jervis Street Hospital. When the GPO was set ablaze on Friday evening, Mac Diarmada took charge of ensuring the orderly evacuation of the building.

Rebel headquarters were established in a house on nearby Moore Street and, when rumours of a surrender began to circulate, Mac Diarmada intervened to settle the angry protests of the rebels. Joe Good, a Volunteer who had returned to Dublin from England to fight in the Rising, recalled Mac Diarmada's clear and persuasive argument that convinced the Volunteers that the time for surrender had come:

> He suggested that we take a long look at the dead civilians lying in the street outside our windows. He asked us to imagine how many more of them would be lying there if we fought on. He also stressed that the civilians nearest us were all very poor and would be butchered with us. He said that the rest of 'this beautiful city' would be razed. 'You've all seen what happened to the Post Office!' He told us the worst that would happen to the Irish Volunteers from England would be a 'few years' in jail. He said we'd 'fought a gallant fight' and we'd only lose now by fighting further. He told us that our only remaining duty now was to survive. ... He ended by insisting quietly, and still smiling, that 'We, who will be shot, will die happy – knowing that there are still plenty of you around who will finish the job.'[14]

Mac Diarmada was with the party of rebels who surrendered at the junction of Henry Street and Sackville Street. Like the other rebels, he spent Saturday night in the open air at the Rotunda Gardens. One of the officers on duty confiscated his walking stick and was said to have remarked, 'You have cripples in your army.'[15]

Mac Diarmada marched to Richmond Barracks at the back of the main party of rebels and was escorted by two Volunteers. Joseph O'Rourke described an incident shortly after they arrived, when Mac Diarmada almost escaped the attention of the authorities. The two were part of a group of twenty-five men who were told on Sunday morning that they were to be deported to England. Just as they were gathering to leave in the barrack square, Mac Diarmada was spotted by a detective in the DMP, Johnny Barton, who said to Mac Diarmada: 'Ah no, Johnny, you're not leaving us. You are to stay here.'[16]

Mac Diarmada was eventually brought to trial on 9 May. Most of the executions had taken place at this point and the authorities were endeavouring to make sure that the remaining rebels were convicted on solid evidence. Six prosecution witnesses testified at Mac Diarmada's court martial. Evidence given against him included his association with the leaders of the Irish Volunteers, his regular presence in Clarke's tobacconist shop and his presence on Parnell Street when the rebels surrendered. Mac Diarmada was found guilty of taking part in an armed rebellion and was sentenced to death by being shot.

Mac Diarmada's death sentence was confirmed swiftly but his execution was delayed for some days as Prime Minister Herbert Asquith attempted to pacify public opinion, which was turning against the executions. As Mac Diarmada was a signatory of the Proclamation, his execution was never in doubt. While he awaited his execution in Kilmainham Gaol, he was not visited by his family members, who mostly lived in Co. Leitrim and in the United States. He wrote a long letter to his brothers and sisters on 11 May, telling them that he felt happiness in the face of death:

The cause for which I die has been rebaptised during the past week by the blood of as good men as ever trod God's earth and should I not feel justly proud to be numbered amongst them. Before God let me again assure you of how proud and happy I feel.[17]

In the days preceding his execution, Mac Diarmada was visited on two occasions by his friend Fr Patrick Browne, a lecturer in Maynooth College. Browne observed that during his first visit Mac Diarmada 'spoke fairly bitterly about the Church'.[18] He criticised its past treatment of Fenians, in particular Charles Kickham, who was refused admittance to a church in Thurles.

The night before his execution Mac Diarmada was visited by sisters Min and Phyllis Ryan from Co. Wexford. Min was Mac Diarmada's girlfriend. They had begun seeing each other shortly after Ryan came to Dublin from London in January 1915 to teach languages. In his last letter to his family, Mac Diarmada wrote that Min 'in all probability ... would have been my wife'.[19] She later married Richard Mulcahy, chief of staff of the Irish Republican Army (IRA) during the War of Independence. The sisters were permitted a three-hour visit from midnight until 3 a.m. and they talked about many topics, staying away from 'the evil moment of asking him anything about what was going to happen'.[20] Before the sisters left, he cut the buttons off his coat to give as souvenirs to relatives and friends. The women left when a priest arrived at 3 a.m. Seán Mac Diarmada was executed in the Stonebreakers' Yard of Kilmainham Gaol at 3.45 a.m. on 12 May 1916.

JAMES CONNOLLY

James Connolly, the socialist leader of the Easter Rising, was born at Cowgate, Edinburgh on 5 June 1868. Cowgate was the Irish ghetto of the city and Connolly endured deprivation and harsh living conditions throughout his childhood. His parents, John and Mary (née McGinn), were from Co. Monaghan. John worked as a manure carter and later as a lamp lighter. His low wages ensured that James did not benefit from a full primary school education and by the age of ten he had already worked as a printer's devil and as a baker's assistant. He was influenced by his older brother John and followed him into the British Army around 1882, when he was just fourteen years old. Connolly was probably fed up with the menial jobs he did in Edinburgh and was attracted by the steady pay of the army. Very few records survive of his service in the King's Liverpool Regiment and although he did not deny his military career in later years, he did not talk about it freely either. Connolly spent a large proportion of his years of service in Ireland and he deserted the army in 1888, returning to Scotland, where he lived in Dundee. His decision to leave may have had to do with the fact that his regiment was due to be sent to India.[1]

It was while living in Dundee that Connolly first came under the influence of socialist thinking. At this time the growth in socialist organisations and trade unions across Scotland was evident in this city in the north-east of the country. Connolly joined the Socialist League in Dundee, where his brother was also a member. Although he had received limited schooling, Connolly was an avid reader and a largely self-educated man. He began to read widely on socialism, including the writings of Karl Marx, and later he joined study groups, where he could discuss the more difficult texts with like-minded individuals.[2]

While serving with the British Army in Dublin, Connolly had met Lillie Reynolds, a Protestant domestic servant from Co. Wicklow. Her granduncle had fought in the 1798 rebellion on the side of the rebels.[3] Connolly came to Scotland a year before they were married so that he could set up home for them both, and the couple were married in Perth in April 1890. Shortly afterwards they moved to Edinburgh, where Connolly confirmed his conversion to socialism through his involvement with the Scottish Socialist Federation (SSF).

While in the SSF he met the secretary of the organisation, John Leslie. Leslie, along with Connolly's brother John, who was by now a leading member of the SSF Edinburgh branch, facilitated Connolly's growing involvement in the socialist politics of the city. Leslie's pamphlet, *The Present Position of the Irish Question*, which addressed the situation regarding Home Rule in Ireland from a socialist point of view, was an inspiration to Connolly. He wrote articles for the journal *Socialist*, took over from his brother as secretary of the SSF in Edinburgh, and in 1894 he was the SSF candidate in the local municipal elections.

Connolly's success in socialist politics in Edinburgh was not mirrored by success in his working life. He lost his job as a carter for Edinburgh council and his efforts to set up a business as a cobbler failed in 1895. He became disillusioned following a heavy defeat in local Poor Law elections in April of that year. For a while he contemplated emigration to Chile, but his wife was not in favour of such a move. Leslie placed an advertisement in *Justice* appealing for work for Connolly and he was offered a job as organiser for the Socialist Club in Dublin, with a salary of £1 per week.

By now Connolly had three daughters, Nora, Mona and Aideen, and in April 1896 the family moved to Dublin, setting up home in a tenement dwelling on Charlemont Street. The number of socialist organisations in Dublin was much smaller than in Edinburgh, and his wages depended on the ability of members to pay their subscriptions. When this did not happen, Connolly often went unpaid. By May Connolly had initiated the establishment of the Irish Socialist Republican Party (ISRP), which aimed to unite socialist and nationalist opinion in Ireland. The organisation began with just eight founding members gathered in a public house on Thomas Street. Although it remained small, some branches were established in other cities in Ireland. The party's manifesto called for the creation of an 'Irish Socialist Republic', where private ownership of land and the means of production would cease.[4]

Over the next few years Connolly developed his thinking on the idea of a socialist Irish republic, publishing various pamphlets and articles on this topic, for example in the newspaper *Labour Leader* and the nationalist literary journal *Shan Van Vocht*. During this period a number of nationalist committees sprang up to organise commemorations of the 1798 rebellion. In January 1897 Connolly published an article in *Shan Van Vocht* entitled 'Nationalism and Socialism', in which he argued that historic commemorations should not replace the need for action on present issues facing Ireland. He wrote that the nationalist movement 'must demonstrate to the people of Ireland that our nationalism is not merely a morbid idealising of the past, but is also capable of formulating a distinct and definite answer to the problems of the present'.[5]

Later that year he organised protests against celebrations for the Diamond Jubilee of Queen Victoria, and in June he was arrested for his involvement in a procession on Jubilee Day, during which a black coffin with the words 'British Empire' inscribed on it was paraded through Dublin. Maud Gonne paid the fine that secured his release from custody.

In 1898, with financial assistance from his mentor, the Scottish labour leader Keir Hardie, Connolly founded the socialist newspaper the *Workers' Republic*. It was intended as a monthly newspaper but its publication was very sporadic. Connolly's aim in founding a newspaper was to provide an alternative to the Home Rule opinion found in most newspapers and to educate people in the kind of thinking that might prompt a socialist revolution.

The ISRP took the lead in starting a campaign for the Boers during the conflict in South Africa in 1899. An ISRP protest meeting held at Foster Place on 21 August 1899 was the first pro-Boer meeting to take place in Ireland. Connolly became a member of the Irish Transvaal Committee, set up by Gonne and Arthur Griffith to help the Boers in their fight.

Connolly often went without pay for his political work and as a result his family lived in poverty. His daughter Ina recalled how her father was more hurt by the fact that his comrades neglected to pay him his due rather than the lack of money itself. She recalled one Christmas when the only toy he brought home for his children was a johnny-dancing-on-a-stick bought from a beggar on Thomas Street, and her mother had to rely on money borrowed from a kindly neighbour to put food on the Christmas table.[6] In 1897 the family moved to another one-room tenement dwelling in Pimlico. Their poverty was a strong factor in Connolly's eventual decision to move to America in 1903.

In the meantime Connolly continued his involvement in socialist politics in Dublin, standing as a candidate in municipal elections. He often faced down bitter opposition during the campaigns and did not poll high. Connolly became increasingly involved in socialism outside Ireland. In 1901 and 1902 he embarked on speaking tours of Scotland and England, enthusing audiences with his simple style of speaking. He played a minor role in an international socialist dispute in 1901 over the decision of a French socialist party to enter government in France. Connolly was also developing links with Daniel De Leon, a key figure in the Socialist Labor Party in America, and with De Leon's assistance he arranged a speaking tour of the USA from autumn 1902 to January 1903.

While in America Connolly became increasingly agitated when he was made aware that back in Dublin the ISRP had delayed the publication of several issues of the *Workers' Republic*. He was infuriated when he discovered that money he had sent home from America to finance the newspaper had been spent on covering a deficit run up by the bar of the party's club room. On his return, Connolly resigned from the party when his motion to pay for the printing costs of the *Workers' Republic*, to avoid the foreclosure of its printing press, was defeated. His decision led to the virtual collapse of the ISRP and in the spring of 1903 Connolly began to contemplate emigrating to America.

Connolly arrived in New York in autumn 1903. His family remained in Dublin; the plan was that Connolly would establish himself in America before Lillie and the children moved over. Although he had hoped to secure employment with the newspaper of the Socialist Labor Party of America, Connolly had to settle for a job as an insurance collector in the town of Troy in upstate New York. He found that he did not agree with the prevailing socialist thinking in America and he frequently came into conflict with American socialist leaders, including De Leon. Although he was by now no longer a practising Catholic, Connolly disagreed with De Leon's belief that it was not possible to be a socialist and hold religious beliefs at the same time. His unhappiness was further compounded by the tragic death of his daughter Mona in a fire shortly before the family were due to join him in America. The day before their departure, Mona's apron caught fire as she was helping out in the home of a family friend and she died in hospital from her burns.

Not long after the family arrived in America they moved to Newark, New Jersey, where Connolly was employed at the Singer sewing machine factory. The International Workers of the World (IWW, also known as 'the Wobblies') was founded in Chicago in 1905. Connolly was attracted by the main aim of the organisation: to unite the various trade unions under a single banner with the aim of overthrowing the capitalist system. He became an organiser for the IWW in the Bronx, New York, and learned to speak Italian fluently so that he could communicate with the large community of immigrant workers from Italy.

But Connolly was equally dedicated to organising the Irish immigrant workers in New York, and in 1907 he founded the Irish Socialist Federation and set up *The Harp* newspaper, which provided him with a platform for his writings. Connolly also kept in touch with what was happening in Ireland and corresponded with William O'Brien, a trade union organiser in Dublin. With O'Brien he arranged for the publication of *The Harp* in Ireland. Eventually O'Brien secured funds to allow Connolly to fulfil his desire to return to Ireland, and he arrived home in July 1910 to begin a lecture tour of the country.

It was also in July 1910 that Connolly published *Labour in Irish History*, a history of Ireland since the late 1600s from a socialist perspective. The book was well received and it demonstrated how Connolly had developed into a skilful Marxist writer capable of presenting centuries of Irish history in a simple and accessible style. In the same month his pamphlet *Labour, Nationality and Religion* was published. This was written in response to a series of anti-socialist lectures published by the Jesuit priest Fr Francis Kane earlier that year. In the pamphlet

Connolly defended the idea that socialism and Catholicism could be compatible and listed numerous examples from Irish history of occasions when the actions of the Catholic Church had interfered with the cause of Irish freedom.

On his return to Ireland Connolly found that the socialist scene had changed greatly since his departure. The arrival of the labour activist James Larkin in Dublin in 1908 and his establishment of the ITGWU reinvigorated trade unionism in the city. The new Socialist Party of Ireland (SPI), founded in August 1909, provided Connolly with an opportunity to re-establish himself in Dublin. He initially embarked on a speaking tour of Ireland, England and Scotland and, when it seemed as if he would gain employment as an organiser with the SPI, his family returned to Ireland in December 1910. But the SPI failed to raise sufficient funds to finance Connolly's position and in 1911 he moved to Belfast, where he became embroiled in the industrial unrest taking place in that city. His involvement in a dockers' dispute – where he negotiated on behalf of 300 dockers who went on strike in sympathy with striking workers in Britain – eventually led to his appointment as secretary of the ITGWU in Belfast. He also organised the female mill workers in the city by setting up a textile union within the ITGWU. However, Connolly was limited in what he could do for the cause of trade unionism by the sectarian divisions in the city between Protestants and Catholics. He could not reconcile himself to the opposition of Protestant socialists in Ulster to Home Rule for Ireland.

One of his most significant achievements during this period occurred at a conference of Irish socialist organisations at the Antient Concert Rooms in Dublin at Easter 1912. Connolly had been working for some time on persuading the various strands of socialism in Ireland to unify as a political party and he succeeded in achieving this goal with the establishment of the Independent Labour Party of Ireland (ILP) at the conference. He had created a political platform for socialists in Ireland, with the ILP eventually leading to the foundation of the Irish Labour Party.

In August 1913 Connolly was summoned from Belfast to Dublin by Larkin to assist with organising workers in the union disputes taking place at that time. This was the beginning of the Dublin Lockout, the major industrial battle of 1913. The clash centred on a conflict between William Martin Murphy, the wealthiest employer in Dublin, and workers in his company, Dublin United Tramways, who wanted to organise themselves as a union. Murphy began to dismiss employees whom he suspected were members of trade unions. The tramway workers responded by striking on 26 August, and in turn Murphy 'locked out' the strikers, replacing them with non-union workers. When Connolly arrived back in Dublin in late August 1913, a gathering of the striking workers due to take place on Sackville Street the following Sunday had been outlawed by the authorities. At a meeting at Beresford Place on 29 August, Larkin burned the notice of the proclamation and Connolly addressed the crowd, encouraging them to disregard the proclamation and to turn out on Sackville Street in any case. Connolly was arrested the next day and so did not witness the riot that occurred on Sackville Street that Sunday. Larkin addressed the crowd from the window of the Imperial Hotel and the police baton-charged the crowd, fatally injuring two men.

Connolly was sentenced to three months' imprisonment but was released on bail after a couple of weeks. Larkin went to England to raise support for the Lockout, leaving Connolly responsible for organising the workers in Dublin. He took charge of the Lockout from late October, when Larkin was sentenced to seven months' imprisonment.

The Lockout lasted for several months, but when Larkin and Connolly failed to convince the Trades Union Congress in Britain to strike in sympathetic action with the workers in Dublin, it lost its momentum. Striking workers returned to work in January 1914 and Larkin left for America later that year, not returning until 1923. In the absence of Larkin, Connolly was appointed acting general secretary of the ITGWU. Connolly's sense of disappointment and disillusionment at the failure of socialist revolution in Ireland was captured in an article in the Scottish newspaper *Forward* in February 1914:

And so we Irish workers must go down into Hell, bow our backs to the lash of the slave driver, let our hearts be seared by the iron of his hatred, and instead of the sacramental wafer of brother-hood and common sacrifice, eat the dust of defeat and betrayal.[7]

The Lockout did have one positive outcome for Connolly. In November 1913 a military organisation, the Irish Citizen Army (ICA), was formed to defend the workers. In the aftermath of the Lockout, Connolly was able to build the ICA into a small revolutionary force that would seek the establishment of a socialist Irish republic.

The outbreak of war in Europe in August 1914 outraged Connolly. Fuelled by anger at what he viewed as the unnecessary slaughter of the working class, Connolly called for a socialist uprising with renewed vigour, writing in August 1914 that 'a great continental uprising of the working class would stop the war'.[8] On 9 September Connolly attended a meeting of key figures from nationalist organisations, including Patrick Pearse, Joseph Plunkett, Éamonn Ceannt and Tom Clarke, at which it was decided to take advantage of England's war with Germany to stage a rebellion in Ireland. From their base at Liberty Hall on the north quays of Dublin city, Connolly continued to drill the ICA. Numbers remained small, at approximately 200, but they were a well-trained force.

Throughout 1914 and 1915 Connolly's speeches and writings became increasingly militant and his call for action grew more forceful. His impatience caused the leadership of the IRB to fear that he and the ICA might go it alone and stage a rebellion without the support of the Irish Volunteers. In January 1916 Connolly was brought to a secret location by senior figures in the IRB and persuaded to hold off until the Irish Volunteers were ready to participate in a joint uprising.

It remains a point of dispute as to whether Connolly was kidnapped to attend this meeting or whether he attended of his own free will. Regardless, the outcome of the meeting was that a provisional date for the Rising was set for Easter 1916 and Connolly was co-opted onto the military committee of the IRB.

When the Rising eventually broke out on Easter Monday 1916, approximately 200 members of the ICA assembled in Liberty Hall. Connolly ordered some of them to take St Stephen's Green under Michael Mallin, others to take City Hall under Seán Connolly and the rest followed him to the GPO, where Connolly was commander of the forces in Dublin. He was accompanied by Winifred Carney, his personal secretary for many years and the only woman to march with the column to the GPO. Compared with Cumann na mBan, whose members' duties during the Rising were confined to cooking meals, nursing the wounded and acting as couriers, a number of women attached to the ICA were permitted to take part in combat. Connolly himself held strong feminist beliefs, although within the ICA 'equality of the sexes ... was an implicit rather than a written dictate'.[9] The most prominent women who took part in the Rising were members of the ICA, including Constance Markievicz, Kathleen Lynn, Elizabeth O'Farrell and Nellie Gifford.

On reaching the GPO that morning, it was Connolly who gave the order to seize the building, shouting 'Left turn! Charge!' As the rebels rushed the building, he took control, giving instructions to evacuate the building, smash windows and erect barricades. In the midst of the chaos his son Roddy remembered seeing his father picking up the handkerchief of a distressed female customer who had dropped it in her haste to leave the building. He presented it to her, behaving 'very courteously even in the midst of leading the revolutionary forces'.[10] Connolly accompanied Pearse outside the GPO for the reading of the Proclamation, which had been printed by the same men who printed *The Workers' Republic*. When Pearse had finished reading the Proclamation, Connolly turned to him and said, 'Thank God, Pearse, we have lived to see this day!'[11]

Throughout Easter Week Connolly showed impressive leadership in the GPO and more than any other leader took charge of giving orders, inspecting positions and communicating with the other outposts via dispatches typed up by Carney. On Tuesday morning Ignatius Callendar was impressed by Connolly's 'remarkable coolness' as he accepted a message from him for Edward Daly at the Four Courts.[12] Connolly kept up the spirits of the Volunteers through his appearance of authority, his optimistic attitude and his words of encouragement, but it was evident that by Wednesday he did not hold out much hope for the GPO garrison. That afternoon he took his son Roddy aside and gave him a suitcase of documents to deliver to his trade union colleague William O'Brien. He told Roddy not to return to the GPO as he anticipated that the British would shortly begin shelling the building.

During Easter Week Connolly often put his personal safety at risk to visit Volunteer outposts in person and frequently left the GPO to deliver instructions to the various barricades in the streets surrounding the post office. On one such occasion on Thursday he led a sortie from the GPO to set up barricades on the western side of the GPO, in the Liffey Street area. On his way back Connolly was wounded in his left leg by rifle fire and was carried back to the GPO on a stretcher. There he received treatment from Dr James Ryan, who identified that Connolly was 'suffering from a severe wound in the ankle. It was badly lacerated, probably from a rifle bullet at comparatively short range.'[13] Thereafter Connolly was less of a physical presence in the GPO, but he continued to provide inspiration. He dictated a message to the Volunteers from his bed, stating in the manifesto issued on Friday morning:

> Courage, boys, we are winning, and in the hour of our victory let us not forget the splendid women who have everywhere stood by us and cheered us on. Never had man or woman a grander cause, never was a cause more grandly served.[14]

When the GPO was evacuated on Friday evening, Connolly stayed until the end, before being carried by stretcher to Moore Street, accompanied by Carney. Seán McLoughlin was one of the stretcher party carrying Connolly out of the GPO, and as they left under heavy fire he overheard Connolly say to Seán Mac Diarmada: 'We have no chance now: this is the end.'[15]

Eventually they reached the new headquarters in Moore Street where the other leaders were gathered, and Connolly was laid on the kitchen floor on his stretcher. At noon the following morning a war council was held around his bed, at which the decision to surrender was taken.

Connolly and the other wounded rebels were brought outside to Moore Street. There they were met by British officers and were then transferred to Dublin Castle, where Connolly was held separately in a small room of the hospital wing. Shortly afterwards he was visited by Major de Courcy Wheeler, staff captain to Brigadier General Lowe, who presented him with Pearse's surrender order and asked him to sign it. Connolly also wrote out his own surrender order for the ICA.

Ina Connolly attempted to visit her father in Dublin Castle on 3 May but was turned away by a nurse who informed her that Connolly was 'very weak from loss of blood'. He was treated for his wounds by surgeons but remained in a poorly condition.[16] On 1 May Connolly asked to see Fr Aloysius, who heard his confession and gave him communion.

Connolly's court martial took place on 9 May 1916 at his hospital bed. The two surgeons who had operated on him certified that he was mentally fit to undergo trial.[17] Four prosecution witnesses were called, all of whom were members of the British military, including de Courcy Wheeler. Connolly made a statement to the court martial, which was later smuggled out by his daughter Nora. In the statement he defended himself against allegations made by two of the witnesses that prisoners were treated in a manner that put their lives in danger. He outlined his rationale for the Easter Rising and what he believed had been achieved:

> We went out to break the connection between this country and the British Empire, and to establish an Irish Republic. We believe that the call we then issued to the people of Ireland was a nobler call, in a holier cause, than any call issued to them during this war, having any connection with the war. We succeeded in proving that Irishmen are ready to die endeavouring to win for Ireland those national rights which the British Government has been asking them to die to win for Belgium. As long as that remains the case, the cause of Irish freedom is safe.[18]

In the early hours of Friday 12 May 1916, Connolly's wife, Lillie, and daughter Nora were brought to see him in Dublin Castle, shortly before he was to be executed, at dawn. It was an emotional final meeting and Lillie broke down towards the end of the visit, saying, 'But your beautiful life, James.' Her husband replied: 'Hasn't it been a full life? Isn't this a good end?'[19] Shortly afterwards James Connolly was brought to Kilmainham Gaol, lying down in an ambulance, still wearing his hospital pyjamas. He was blindfolded and carried into the Stonebreakers' Yard directly, via a gate facing onto Inchicore Road. Connolly faced the firing squad sitting in a chair. He was the last of the leaders of the 1916 Rising to be executed at Kilmainham Gaol.

ROGER CASEMENT

Roger Casement, the only leader of the Easter Rising whose execution took place outside Ireland, was born in Sandycove, Dublin, on 1 September 1864. He was raised as a Protestant, although Casement and his siblings – brothers Charlie and Tom and sister Agnes (known as Nina) – were secretly baptised as Catholics by their mother, Anne. By the time Casement was thirteen years old both his parents had died and the children were cared for by relatives, including his Uncle John at his house Magheratemple, near Ballycastle, Co.

Antrim. He attended a local diocesan school in Ballymena as a boarder and spent much of his teenage years walking the Glens of Antrim and learning about local history, in particular the events of the 1798 rebellion.[1] Although Casement moved around frequently during his childhood and never settled in one place throughout his adult life, he 'was always to think of himself as an Ulsterman'.[2]

As a young man Casement often visited his Liverpool cousins, the Bannisters. His mother's sister, Grace, was married to Edward Bannister, an agent for companies who traded in West Africa. Bannister helped to secure a position for Casement with the Elder Dempster shipping company, and he embarked on a journey to the port town of Boma in the Congo in 1884. This trip provided him with his first taste of what was then known as the Dark Continent and marked the beginning of Casement's twenty years of travel and exploration in Africa.

When he arrived in the Congo Casement offered his services to the Congo International Association, an organisation funded by King Leopold II of Belgium and run by the renowned British explorer Henry Stanley. The Berlin Conference in 1885 led to the creation of the Congo Free State under Belgian influence. The challenge facing a group of European men in the Congo, including Casement, was to explore, develop and exploit the resources of this vast and mostly unchartered area of land. From 1884 to 1889 Casement worked in a number of positions in the Congo. He was organiser of supplies for Henry Sandford's expedition to unexplored areas of the territory, worked as a surveyor for a proposed railway line and volunteered as a lay missionary. During this period in the Congo Casement met the writer Joseph Conrad, later author of the renowned novel *Heart of Darkness*, an account of the journey of Charles Marlow down the Congo River. Casement made a strong impression on Conrad, whom he described as a man who 'thinks, speaks well, [is] most intelligent and very sympathetic'.[3]

Casement left Africa in late 1889 to accompany Herbert Ward on a speaking tour of America, but returned in 1892 to take up a position as customs officer and surveyor in the Niger Coast protectorate. His work brought him to the attention of the British consular service, and in 1895 he was appointed consul to the city of Lourenço Marques in Portuguese East Africa, now Mozambique. One of his main duties was to report on the movement of arms by the Boers of the Transvaal through Lourenço Marques. Following an extended period of home leave in 1898 Casement was sent as consul to Luanda in Portuguese West Africa, covering an extensive area that included Angola and the Congo Free State.

In June 1903 Casement left Matadi, a seaport in the western region of the Congo, to begin a steamboat journey upriver to the interior of the country. His travels were sanctioned by the Foreign Office and he made the journey to investigate allegations of the mistreatment of native Congolese working in the rubber trade. The extraction of rubber had proved extremely lucrative for Belgian companies controlled by King Leopold, as rubber was a highly valued commodity on international markets. Casement spent several months investigating the exploitation of the rubber workers and the atrocities carried out against the native people of that region, and his report on the Congo was published by the British government in 1904, causing international outrage. He exposed a litany of abuses. Workers were being forced to travel deep into the forests to gather rubber for a pittance and were flogged, mutilated or even killed if they failed to return with sufficient amounts.

Casement spent most of 1904 in Ireland, where he began to associate with the Irish Ireland movement through his involvement with organisations such as the Gaelic League and his developing relationships with prominent figures in nationalist circles. However, as highlighted by Brian Inglis, Casement was 'not at this stage a rebel' and his politics were closer to Home Rule than republicanism.[4] In June 1904 Casement attended the Feis of the Glens in Co. Antrim, a festival of Irish language and culture, and here he met Bulmer Hobson, then a young activist in the GAA and Gaelic League. Hobson recalled that Casement was 'intensely interested' in the nationalist groups forming around that time and offered to help in whatever way he could.[5] He made generous donations to Irish language causes, including the Gaeltacht peninsula of Tawin in Connacht and Patrick Pearse's school, St Enda's, in Dublin.

Casement was attracted to Arthur Griffith's ideas on dual monarchy and economic self-sufficiency, which he read about in Griffith's paper the *United Irishman*, and he subsequently contributed articles to that newspaper himself. It was during this period that he developed a friendship with the historian Alice Stopford Green and they corresponded with each other about their shared interests in Irish history and colonial policy.

In 1906 Casement received another posting from the Foreign Office, this time to Santos, Brazil. He was unhappy there and seemed preoccupied by the progress of the nationalist movement at home in Ireland. He wrote to his cousin Gertrude Bannister: 'I am a queer sort of consul … I really ought to be in jail instead of under the Lion and the Unicorn.'[6] He was transferred to Belém do Pará in 1908, which gave him his first opportunity to explore the Amazonian rainforest, and in 1909 he reached the high point of his diplomatic career when he was appointed British consul general at Rio de Janeiro.

While on leave in Ireland in June 1910 Casement was approached by the Anti-Slavery and Aborigines Protection Society and asked to investigate rumours of ill-treatment of indigenous people and workers from Barbados employed by the Peruvian Amazon Company to collect rubber. In July he embarked on a commission of inquiry facilitated by the Peruvian Amazon Company, travelling upriver to Putumayo. Through his investigations Casement identified what he described as 'a conspiracy of evil'.[7] His findings were shockingly similar to the gruesome discoveries he had made in the Congo: workers were subjected to floggings, torture and sexual abuse, and mass killings occurred. His reports for the Foreign Office were eventually published and Casement presented his findings to the US president, William Taft. He received a knighthood for his work in 1911, which he accepted with some reluctance owing to his developing sense of Irish nationalism.

Casement resigned from the Foreign Office in 1913 and was quickly taken up with the political crisis that occurred in Ireland that year over the proposed introduction of Home Rule. Casement believed it was still possible to persuade unionists to support Irish nationalism. In October he organised a meeting of Ulster Protestants in Ballymoney, Co. Antrim, at which speakers 'tried to assuage fears of home rule'.[8] The meeting itself was a success, but such was the strength of opposition to Home Rule in Ulster that the meeting had little impact on public opinion.

In November 1913 Eoin MacNeill's article 'The North Began', published in *An Claidheamh Soluis*, prompted the formation of the Irish Volunteers to defend the introduction of Home Rule in Ireland. MacNeill, like Casement, was from Co. Antrim and the pair had been friends for some time. The involvement of another friend, Bulmer Hobson, ensured that Casement became a member of the Provisional Committee of the Irish Volunteers. Casement was sent to London to explain the purpose of the Irish Volunteers to the press and he spent the following months travelling around Ireland recruiting members for the organisation.

Casement saw the arming of the Volunteers as necessary if the organisation was to fulfil its function and defend Home Rule. To this end, he and a number of friends, including Hobson, Stopford Green, Erskine Childers and Darrell Figgis, organised the importation of arms purchased in Belgium. The weapons were transported in Childers' yacht, the *Asgard*, and landed at Howth on 26 July 1914. Casement realised that limited funds and lack of weapons in Ireland would prevent the Volunteers from arming themselves any further. He decided that the large emigrant community in America could help, and by the time of the Howth gun-running he was already in Philadelphia, seeking financial support and weapons for the Irish Volunteers. However, the outbreak of the war in Europe shortly after Casement's arrival in America diverted attention from the cause of the Irish Volunteers and Casement struggled to raise funds.

The leaders of the Irish-American nationalist organisation Clan na Gael had begun discussions with German contacts in the USA about the possibility of using German support to overthrow British rule in Ireland while the war was ongoing. Casement became drawn towards this course of action and in October 1914 he left America for Norway with the intention of making his way to Germany. A letter from Casement published in the *Irish Independent* shortly before his departure brought him to the attention of Foreign Office officials. In the letter Casement argued:

Let Irishmen and boys stay in Ireland. Their duty is clear – before God and before man. We, as a people, have no quarrel with the German people. Germany has never wronged Ireland, and we owe her more than one debt of gratitude.[9]

From the time of his arrival in Oslo, British intelligence kept Casement's activities in Europe under surveillance.

Casement's decision to go to Germany was taken on his own initiative. Tom Clarke's wife, Kathleen, recalled that 'he did not consult any of the revolutionary group' before his departure.[10] On arrival in Berlin, he was received by Count Artur von Zimmermann, the undersecretary of state. After a positive meeting with him, Casement drafted a set of proposals for the German government, which included the formation of an Irish Brigade among prisoners of war from Ireland held in German camps. This force was to fight for the cause of Irish freedom and would be independent of the German army. On 20 November 1914 an official statement, authorised by the chancellor, was issued by the German government. It gave assurances that 'under no circumstances would Germany invade Ireland with a view to its conquest' and stated that if German forces were to arrive in Ireland during the war they would not be 'an army of invaders' but would only desire 'national prosperity and freedom' for Ireland.[11]

This declaration and a 'treaty' agreed between Germany and Ireland one month later represented an initial triumph for Casement, but the rest of his time in Germany was less successful, as he failed to recruit sufficient numbers to the Irish Brigade. Approximately 2,500 Irish prisoners of war were transferred to a single camp in the town of Limburg, near Frankfurt. Of this number just fifty-six were successfully recruited into the brigade. Arriving in the camp to recruit for the Irish Brigade, Casement and his assistant Michael Kehoe, brigade lieutenant, soon realised that they 'would have a very hard battle to prove to the Irish that there was any necessity to do something to help the Irish Volunteers in Ireland'.[12] Many of the prisoners were still swayed by the arguments that had convinced them to join the British Army in the first place; others feared the consequences of joining a brigade supported by the German government and Casement's cause was not helped by parcels of food and money sent to the prisoners at Limburg by the various societies supporting the war effort at home. Not even the arrival of Joseph Plunkett to the camp could significantly boost the number of recruits.

The failure to muster a significant Irish Brigade left Casement feeling depressed, lonely and unwell. In October 1915 Robert Monteith, a former sergeant major in the British Army and a drill instructor for the Irish Volunteers, arrived in Germany at the behest of Tom Clarke. He trained the fifty-six recruits to the Irish Brigade in a separate camp at Zossen. But the size of the brigade meant that the Germans gave limited support to it and Casement became despondent about their lack of commitment to assist with a rebellion in Ireland. He felt increasingly isolated as it was difficult for him to communicate with the rebellion organisers in Dublin, and John Devoy, the leader of Clan na Gael in America, lost faith in Casement over his inability to recruit an Irish Brigade.

In February 1916 Casement learned that a rebellion was to take place in Ireland at Easter and the Germans committed to sending Casement to Ireland in a submarine, with a small quantity of arms to be transported by ship. Casement knew that without an Irish Brigade or sufficient arms there was little hope of a successful rebellion, and his aim in travelling back to Ireland was mostly to try to prevent an uprising from taking place.

Casement's submarine and the arms ship, the *Aud*, travelled separately to Ireland, where they intended to rendezvous in Tralee Bay on Good Friday 1916. Although both the *Aud* and Casement's U-boat successfully made it to their destination on the appointed date, poor communication and a series of misunderstandings meant that the boats failed to make contact with one another. Casement and his companions, Monteith and Daniel Bailey, left the U-boat in a small dinghy. They struggled to reach the Co. Kerry shoreline and their boat even capsized at one point, but eventually they landed on Banna Strand in the early hours of 21 April. Casement collapsed on the beach, completely exhausted. Monteith and Bailey went to seek the assistance of the Volunteers in Tralee, but in the meantime Casement was discovered by RIC officers who had been alerted to suspicious activities taking place on the beach. He was arrested and held that night in Tralee Gaol.

The next day Casement was transferred to London, where he was interrogated at Scotland Yard by senior officials from British intelligence. On Easter Monday, as the Rising broke out in Dublin, Casement was being held in the Tower of London. By this point the authorities were in possession of Casement's diaries, known as the 'Black Diaries', which contained explicit details of Casement's homosexual relationships. The debate continues over the authenticity of the diaries, with some historians arguing that they were forgeries. Whether the diaries were genuine or not, their contents were circulated widely among the British establishment and were used with great effect to discredit even further Casement's tarnished reputation.

Unlike the rest of the men executed for their involvement in the Rising, Casement was tried for high treason under a statute dating from the reign of Edward III in 1351. The trial opened at the Old Bailey on 26 June, where he was represented by the barrister A. M. Sullivan. Sullivan argued in Casement's defence that the 1351 statute was restricted to acts of treason committed by 'the King's enemies in his realm'.[13] Therefore, as Casement's treasonous acts were committed outside the realm of the king, he could not be convicted for them. Witnesses who testified at the trial included soldiers from the Limburg camp and people who had seen Casement at Banna Strand on Good Friday. After four days, Casement was found guilty of high treason. He was allowed to make a speech from the dock, in which he commented on the absurdity of being tried under a medieval statute and expressed his desire to be tried in a court in Ireland. He considered that his act of loyalty to his country had been confused as an act of treachery and he made a passionate defence of the right to independence of the Irish:

> Self-government is our right, a thing born in us at birth; a thing no more to be doled out to us or withheld from us by another

people than the right to life itself – than the right to feel the sun or smell the flowers, or to love our kind. It is only from the convict these things are withheld for crimes committed and proven – and, Ireland, that has wronged no man, that has injured no land, that has sought no dominion over others – Ireland is treated today among the nations of the world as if she were a convicted criminal. If it be treason to fight against such an unnatural fate as this, then I am proud to be a rebel, and shall cling to my 'rebellion' with the last drop of my blood.[14]

Casement was held in Pentonville Prison while awaiting his execution. The day after his conviction he was stripped of his knighthood. An appeal was put forward immediately and his influential friends in Britain and Ireland began a campaign for clemency, but a reprieve was not forthcoming, and the appeal, heard on 17 and 18 July, was unsuccessful. The day before his execution Casement was officially baptised into the Catholic Church.

Unique among the executed leaders of the Easter Rising, Roger Casement was sentenced to death by hanging. He was executed at Pentonville on 3 August 1916 and buried in the grounds of the prison. His remains were transferred to Ireland in 1965 and re-interred in Glasnevin cemetery.

ENDNOTES

INTRODUCTION

1   Matthews, A., *Renegades: Irish Republican Women 1900–1922* (Mercier Press, Cork, 2010), p. 336.

2   Foy, M. T. and Barton, B., *The Easter Rising* (The History Press, Gloucestershire, 2011), p. 294.

PATRICK PEARSE

1   Crowley, B., '"I am the son of a good father": James and Patrick Pearse', in Higgins, R. and Uí Chollatáin, R. (eds), *The Life and After-life of P. H. Pearse* (Irish Academic Press, Dublin, 2009), p. 11.

2   Pearse, P., 'Fragment of Autobiography', Pearse Museum, PMSTE.2003.0946.

3   Pearse, M. B., *The Home Life of Padraig Pearse: As Told by Himself, His Family, His Friends* (Mercier Press, Dublin and Cork, 1979), p. 11.

4   Augusteijn, J., *Patrick Pearse: The Making of a Revolutionary* (Palgrave Macmillan, London, 2010), p. 37.

5   Dudley Edwards, R., *Patrick Pearse: The Triumph of Failure* (Faber & Faber, London, 1977), p. 26.

6   Pearse, P., 'Education in the West of Ireland', quoted in Ó Buachalla, S. (ed.), *A Significant Irish Educationalist: The Educational Writings of P. H. Pearse* (Mercier Press, Dublin and Cork, 1980), pp. 313–14.

7   Reddin, K., 'A Man Called Pearse', *Studies*, vol. 34, no. 134, 1945, pp. 244–5.

8   Ryan, D., *Remembering Sion: A Chronicle of Storm and Quiet* (Arthur Barker, London, 1934), p. 126.

9   Pearse, P., 'The Coming Revolution', *An Claidheamh Soluis,* 8 November 1913.

10   FitzGerald, D., *Desmond's Rising: Memoirs 1913 to Easter 1916* (Liberties Press, Dublin, 2006), pp. 135, 139.

11   *Sinn Féin Rebellion Handbook* (The Weekly Irish Times, Dublin, 1917), p. 50.

12   Bureau of Military History (BMH) WS 249, Frank Henderson, p. 54.

13   Mac Lochlainn, P. F., *Last Words: Letters and Statements of the Leaders Executed after the Rising at Easter 1916* (Government of Ireland, Dublin, 2005), p. 14.

14   Barton, B., *The Secret Court Martial Records of the Easter Rising* (The History Press, Gloucestershire, 2010), p. 131.

15   BMH WS 200, Father Aloysius.

THOMAS CLARKE

1   MacAtasney, G., *Tom Clarke: Life, Liberty, Revolution* (Merrion, Dublin, 2012), p. 3.

2   BMH WS 368, Seán McGarry, p. 1.

3   BMH WS 226, William J. Kelly, p. 1.

4   Le Roux, L. N., *Tom Clarke and the Irish Freedom Movement* (Talbot Press, Dublin, 1936), p. 23.

5   Clarke, T., *Glimpses of an Irish Felon's Prison Life* (Maunsel and Roberts, Dublin, 1922), p. 2.

6   *Ibid.*, p. 6.

7   Clarke, K. (author) and Litton, H. (ed.), *Kathleen Clarke: Revolutionary Woman* (O'Brien Press, Dublin, 1991), p. 24.

8   BMH WS 368, Seán McGarry, p. 16.

9   Foy and Barton (2011), p. 20.

10 Clarke and Litton (1991), p. 52.

11 MacAtasney (2012), p. 85.

12 BMH WS 368, Seán McGarry, p. 17.

13 Clarke and Litton (1991), p. 69.

14 BMH WS 368, Seán McGarry, p. 23.

15 *Ibid.*, p. 24.

16 BMH WS 399, Min Mulcahy (née Ryan), pp. 15–16.

17 Clarke and Litton (1991), p. 83.

18 Mac Lochlainn (2005), p. 44.

19 Clarke and Litton (1991), p. 93.

Thomas MacDonagh

1   Parks, E. W. and Parks, A. W., *Thomas MacDonagh: The Man, the Patriot, the Writer* (University of Georgia Press, Athens, 1967), p. 5.

2   Ryan (1934), p. 17.

3   Norstedt, J. A., *Thomas MacDonagh: A Critical Biography* (University of Virginia Press, Charlottesville, 1980), p. 26.

4   Parks and Parks (1967), p. 9.

5   Ryan (1934), p. 94.

6   RTÉ documentary (1966), *Portraits 1916: Thomas MacDonagh.*

7   *Ibid.*

8   Stephens, J. (ed.), *The Poetical Works of Thomas MacDonagh* (T. Fisher Unwin Ltd, London, 1917), p. ix.

9   Plunkett Dillon, G. (author) and Ó Brolcháin, H. (ed.), *All in the Blood: A Memoir of the Plunkett Family, the 1916 Rising and the War of Independence* (A&A Farmar, Dublin, 2006), p. 107.

10 National Library of Ireland (NLI), Thomas MacDonagh Papers, MS 8,903/1, Thomas MacDonagh to Gertrude Bloomer, 17 June 1910.

11   MacDonagh, T., 'Marching Song of the Irish Volunteers', *The Irish Review*, vol. 3, no. 34, December 1913, pp. 500–2.

12   *The Irish Review*, September–November 1914.

13   Parks and Parks (1967), p. 50.

14   BMH WS 360, Seamus Daly, p. 23.

15   BMH WS 532, John MacDonagh, p. 7.

16   BMH WS 312, Seosamh de Brún, p. 5.

17   *Ibid.*, p. 18.

18   Mac Lochlainn (2005), pp. 55–6.

19   *Ibid.*, p. 61.

Edward Daly

1   Litton, H., *Edward Daly: 16 Lives* (O'Brien Press, Dublin, 2013), p. 23.

2   Mulcahy, D., 'Life and Death of Commandant Edward Daly', in Ó Conchubhair, B. (ed.), *Limerick's Fighting Story 1916–21* (Mercier Press, Cork, 2009), p. 56.

3   Litton (2013), p. 42.

4   Clarke and Litton (1991), p. 44.

5   *Ibid.*, p. 48.

6   BMH WS 259, Brighid Thornton, p. 2.

7   *Ibid.*

8   Stephenson, P. J., 'Heuston's Fort', http://www.1916-rising.com/3-heustonsfort.html.

9   Ó Conchubhair, B. (ed.), *Dublin's Fighting Story 1916–21* (Mercier Press, Cork, 2009), p. 206.

10   BMH WS 393, Séamus S. O'Sullivan, p. 7.

11   O'Brien, P., *Crossfire: The Battle of the Four Courts, 1916* (New Island Books, Dublin, 2012), p. 31.

12   BMH WS 923, Ignatius Callendar, p. 21.

13   Ó Conchubhair, *Limerick's Fighting Story* (2009), p. 107.

14   BMH WS 189, Michael Soughley, p. 2.

15   Barton (2010), p. 171.

16   Mac Lochlainn (2005), p. 70.

WILLIAM PEARSE

1   Pearse (1979), p. 17.

2   Ryan (1934), p. 104.

3   Augusteijn (2010), p. 206.

4   Pearse (1979), p. 54.

5   NLI, Pearse Papers, MS 21,072.

6   Ryan (1934), p. 114.

7   Andrews, C. S., *Dublin Made Me* (Lilliput Press, Dublin, 2001), p. 44.

8   NLI, Pearse Papers, MS 21,072.

9   Ryan (1934), p. 127.

10   BMH WS 694, Frank Burke, p. 4.

11   BMH WS 340, Oscar Traynor, p. 5.

12   Mac Lochlainn (2005), p. 75.

13   *Ibid.*

14   BMH WS 638, Patrick Caldwell, pp. 9–10.

15   BMH WS 1052, Seán MacEntee, p. 114.

16   Mac Lochlainn (2005), p. 77.

17   BMH WS 288, Charles Saurin, p. 49.

18   Mac Lochlainn (2005), p. 80.

19   Barton (2010), p. 179.

20   *Ibid.*, p. 181.

21   BMH WS 200, Fr Aloysius.

Michael O'Hanrahan

1   Tracy, A., 'Michael O'Hanrahan', *Carloviana: The Journal of the Old Carlow Society* (December 1963), p. 13.

2   National Archives of Ireland (NAI), Census of Ireland 1911, 'Residents of a house 21 in Tullow Street (Carlow, Carlow)'.

3   O'Flanagan, Rev. M., Preface to O'Hanrahan, M., *Irish Heroines: Being a Lecture Written for and Delivered before An Árd Craobh Chumann na mBan, Dublin, during the Winter Preceding Easter Week, 1916* (O'Hanrahan family, Dublin, 1917).

4   BMH WS 848, Henry Phibbs, p. 11.

5   NAI, Census of Ireland 1911, 'Residents of a house 67 in Connaught Street (Glasnevin, Dublin)'.

6   BMH WS 848, Henry Phibbs, p. 12.

7   *Ibid.*, p. 11.

8   O'Hanrahan, M., *When the Normans Came* (Browne & Nolan, Dublin, 1931), p. viii.

9   BMH WS 1108, Jeremiah Joseph O'Leary, p. 10.

10   BMH WS 270, Eily O'Hanrahan O'Reilly, pp. 2–3.

11   *Ibid.*, p. 8.

12   BMH WS 995, Bob Price, 'The Surrender of Jacob's Garrison 1916', p. 1.

13   Mac Lochlainn (2005), p. 83.

14   Barton (2010), p. 187.

15   Clarke and Litton (1991), p. 119.

16   BMH WS 270, Eily O'Hanrahan O'Reilly, p. 11.

17   BMH WS 920, Fr Augustine, p. 21.

Joseph Plunkett

1   Plunkett Dillon and Ó Brolcháin (2006), p. 62.

2   BMH WS 488, Jack Plunkett, p. 17.

3   Plunkett Dillon and Ó Brolcháin (2006), p. 107.

4   Ó Brolcháin, H., *Joseph Plunkett: 16 Lives* (O'Brien Press, Dublin, 2012), p. 227.

5   BMH WS 358, Geraldine Dillon, p. 1.

6   *Irish Review,* vol. 4, no. 42, September–November 1914, p. 338.

7   BMH WS 358, Geraldine Dillon, pp. 3–4.

8   Matthews, A., *The Kimmage Garrison, 1916: Making Billy-can Bombs at Larkfield* (Four Courts Press, Dublin, 2010), pp. 19–20.

9   BMH WS 257, Grace Plunkett, p. 1.

10   Ó Brolcháin (2012), p. 353.

11   Townshend, C., *Easter 1916: The Irish Rebellion* (Penguin, London, 2006), p. 123.

12   BMH WS 488, Jack Plunkett, p. 15.

13   BMH WS 388, Joe Good, p. 6.

14   FitzGerald (2006), p. 141.

15   Good, J. (author) and Good, M. (ed.), *Enchanted by Dreams: The Journal of a Revolutionary* (Brandon Books, Dingle, 1996), p. 50.

16   Mac Lochlainn (2005), pp. 91–2.

17   *Ibid.,* p. 93.

18   Barton (2010), p. 208.

19   BMH WS 358, Geraldine Dillon, p. 23.

20   BMH WS 257, Grace Plunkett, p. 11.

21   Mac Lochlainn (2005), pp. 96–7.

John MacBride

1   Jordan, A. J., *Major John MacBride 1865–68* (Westport Historical Society, Westport, 1991), pp. 1–3.

2   NLI, Fred Allan Papers, MS 29,817, John MacBride notebook.

3   *Ibid.*

4   *Ibid.*

5   *The Freeman's Journal*, 27 October 1906.

6   NLI, MS 29,817, John MacBride notebook.

7   Barton (2010), p. 222.

8   BMH WS 219, John MacDonagh, Part 2: 'Notes on a Conversation with John MacDonagh', p. 1.

9   *Ibid.*, Part 1, p. 2.

10   Ó Conchubhair, *Dublin's Fighting Story* (2009), p. 81.

11   BMH WS 532, John MacDonagh, p. 10; BMH WS 312, Seosamh de Brún, p. 6.

12   BMH WS 335, Joseph Furlong, p. 8.

13   Mac Lochlainn (2005), p. 103.

SEÁN HEUSTON

1   Gibney, J., *Seán Heuston: 16 Lives* (O'Brien Press, Dublin, 2013), p. 32.

2   NAI, Census of Ireland 1911, 'Residents of a house 34.4 in Jervis Street (North City, Dublin)'.

3   NLI, MS 10,076.

4   Ó Conchubhair, *Limerick's Fighting Story* (2009), p. 75.

5   *Ibid.*

6   *Ibid.*

7   Gibney (2013), p. 55.

8   BMH WS 1420, Patrick Whelan, p. 2.

9   BMH WS 755, Seán Prendergast, p. 64.

10   *Ibid.*, p. 70.

11   Stephenson, P. J., 'Heuston's Fort', http://www.1916-rising.com/3-heustonsfort.html.

12   BMH CD 309/01, Fr J. M. Heuston OP collection, pp. 5–6.

13   BMH WS 284, Michael Staines, p. 8.

14   Stephenson, http://www.1916-rising.com/3-heustonsfort.html.

15   BMH WS 290, Seán McLoughlin, p. 8.

16   BMH CD 309/01, Fr J. M. Heuston OP collection, pp. 23–4.

17   *Ibid.*, p. 5.

18   *Ibid.*

19   Mac Lochlainn (2005), p. 111.

20   BMH CD 309/01, Fr J. M. Heuston OP collection.

21   Kilmainham Gaol Museum, Seán Heuston Papers.

MICHAEL MALLIN

1   BMH WS 382, Thomas Mallin, p. 1.

2   Hughes, B., *Michael Mallin: 16 Lives* (O'Brien Press, Dublin, 2012), pp. 20–1.

3   BMH WS 382, Thomas Mallin, p. 2.

4   Hughes (2012), p. 36.

5   Kilmainham Gaol Museum, John Hanratty Papers.

6   Mallin, S., 'Micheál Ó Mealláin: An Dromadóir Airm', *Inniu*, 30 September 1966.

7   *Ibid.*, 7 October 1966.

8   Hughes (2012), p. 58.

9   BMH WS 733, James O'Shea, p. 2.

10   *Ibid.*, p. 7.

11   *Ibid.*, p. 8.

12   *Ibid.*

13   Connolly-O'Brien, N., *Portrait of a Rebel Father* (Talbot Press, Dublin, 1935), p. 223.

14   Kilmainham Gaol Museum, John Hanratty Papers.

15   BMH WS 382, Thomas Mallin, p. 4.

16   BMH WS 256, Nellie Gifford Donnelly, p. 3.

17   Hughes (2012), p. 154.

18   BMH WS 585, Frank Robbins, p. 81.

19   Barton (2010), p. 285.

20   Mac Lochlainn (2005), p. 121.

Éamonn Ceannt

1   NLI, Papers of Éamonn and Áine Ceannt, MS 41,479/8, 'Eamonn Ceannt – An Impression' by J. Monks.

2   Henry, W., *Supreme Sacrifice: The Story of Éamonn Ceannt* (Mercier Press, Cork, 2012), p. 33.

3   NLI, Ceannt papers, MS 41,479/8, 'What I Remember About Éamonn' by M. Kent.

4   BMH WS 264, Áine Ceannt, p. 75.

5   NLI, Ceannt papers, MS 41,479/8, 'Eamonn Ceannt's Visit to Rome' by P. J. Daniels.

6   Ó Conchubhair, *Dublin's Fighting Story* (2009), p. 189.

7   BMH WS 264, Áine Ceannt, p. 12.

8   *Ibid.*, p. 22.

9   O'Brien, P., *Uncommon Valour: 1916 and the Battle for the South Dublin Union* (Mercier Press, Cork, 2010), p. 47.

10   BMH WS 304, James Coughlan, p. 16.

11   NLI, Ceannt papers, MS 41,479/1, Lily O'Brennan's account of the activities of the 4th Battalion during Easter Week.

12   *Ibid.*

13   Barton (2010), pp. 238–40.

14   BMH WS 264, Áine Ceannt, p. 34.

15   Mac Lochlainn (2005), p. 136.

Con Colbert

1   NAI, Census of Ireland 1911, 'Residents of a house 7.2 in

Clifton Terrace (Rathmines & Rathgar East, Dublin)'.

2   Daly, M., 'Con Colbert of Athea Hero and Martyr', in Ó Conchubhair, *Limerick's Fighting Story* (2009), p. 70.

3   BMH WS 328, Garry Holohan, p. 11.

4   Ó Conchubhair, *Limerick's Fighting Story* (2009), p. 71.

5   Ryan (1934), p. 166.

6   BMH WS 856, Elizabeth Colbert, p. 6.

7   BMH WS 328, Garry Holohan, p. 34.

8   Clarke and Litton (1991), p. 68.

9   BMH WS 280, Robert Holland, p. 5.

10   Ó Conchubhair, *Limerick's Fighting Story* (2009), p. 72.

11   BMH WS 280, Robert Holland, p. 10.

12   BMH WS 805, Annie Cooney-O'Brien, p. 4.

13   *Ibid.*, p. 5.

14   BMH WS 280, Robert Holland, p. 42.

15   *Ibid.*, p. 46.

16   BMH WS 805, Annie Cooney-O'Brien, p. 13.

17   Mac Lochlainn (2005), p. 151.

18   *Ibid.*

Thomas Kent

1   NAI, Census of Ireland 1911, 'Residents of a house at Coole Lower, Fermoy, Co. Cork'.

2   *Catholic Bulletin* (August 1916), p. 457.

3   BMH WS 75, William Kent, p. 1.

4   BMH WS 1698, Liam de Róiste, p. 264.

5   *Catholic Bulletin* (August 1916), p. 457.

6   BMH WS 75, William Kent, p. 1.

7   BMH WS 1698, Liam de Róiste, p. 278.

8   BMH WS 635, Frank King, p. 1.

9   BMH WS 75, William Kent, p. 2.

10   BMH WS 635, Frank King, p. 2.

11   BMH WS 75, William Kent, p. 2.

12   BMH WS 635, Frank King, p. 4.

13   Barton (2010), p. 298.

Seán Mac Diarmada

1   MacAtasney, G., *Seán Mac Diarmada: Mind of the Revolution* (Drumlin Publications, Manorhamilton, 2004), p. 7.

2   Travers, Rev. C. J., 'Seán Mac Diarmada 1883–1916', *Breifne: Journal of Cumann Seanchais Breifne*, vol. 3, no. 9, 1966, pp. 2–3.

3   *Ibid.*

4   MacAtasney (2004), p. 21.

5   Clarke and Litton (1991), p. 40.

6   BMH WS 914, Denis McCullough, p. 6.

7   BMH WS 755, Seán Prendergast, p. 27.

8   MacAtasney (2004), p. 55.

9   BMH WS 1330, John D. Costello, pp. 3–4.

10   BMH WS 153, Éamonn Dore, p. 5.

11   BMH WS 1364, Dr Catherine J. Quinlan, p. 2.

12   BMH WS 192, Fionán Lynch, p. 11 (typed version).

13   Foy and Barton (2011), p. 188.

14   Good and Good (1996), p. 69.

15   MacAtasney (2004), p. 123.

16   BMH WS 1244, Joseph O'Rourke, p. 13.

17   Mac Lochlainn (2005), p. 169.

18   BMH WS 729, Fr Patrick Browne, p. 7.

19   Mac Lochlainn (2005), p. 170.

20   *Ibid.*, p. 172.

James Connolly

1   Nevin, D., *James Connolly: A Full Life* (Gill & Macmillan, Dublin, 2005), p. 17.

2   Dudley Edwards, R., *James Connolly* (Gill & Macmillan, Dublin, 1981), p. 5.

3   BMH WS 919, Ina Heron, p. 2.

4   Greaves, C. D., *The Life and Times of James Connolly* (Lawrence and Wishart, London, 1986), pp. 75–7.

5   *Shan Van Vocht*, January 1897.

6   BMH WS 919, Ina Heron, pp. 8–9.

7   Connolly, J., *Forward*, 9 February 1914.

8   *Ibid.*, 15 August 1914.

9   Matthews (2010), p. 105.

10 RTÉ documentary (1966), *Portraits 1916: James Connolly*.

11 BMH WS 724, Desmond Ryan, p. 9.

12 BMH WS 923, Ignatius Callendar, p. 9.

13 Mac Lochlainn (2005), p. 179.

14 *Ibid.*, pp. 181–2.

15 BMH WS 290, Seán McLoughlin, p. 22.

16 Mac Lochlainn (2005), p. 187.

17 Barton (2010), p. 338.

18 Mac Lochlainn (2005), pp. 188–9.

19 BMH WS 286, Nora Connolly O'Brien, p. 51.

Roger Casement

1   Mitchell, A., *Roger Casement: 16 Lives* (O'Brien Press, Dublin, 2013), p. 26.

2   Inglis, B., *Roger Casement* (Penguin, London, 2002), p. 23.

3   Hawkins, H., 'Joseph Conrad, Roger Casement and the Congo

Reform Movement', *Journal of Modern Literature* (1981–2), vol. 9, no. 1, p. 67.

4   Inglis (2002), p. 112.

5   BMH WS 1365, Bulmer Hobson, p. 3.

6   Inglis (2002), p. 152.

7   Ó Síocháin, S., *Roger Casement: Imperialist, Rebel, Revolutionary* (Lilliput Press, Dublin, 2008), p. 277.

8   Laffan, M., 'The Making of a Revolutionary: Casement and the Volunteers, 1913–14', in Daly, M. (ed.), *Roger Casement in Irish and World History* (Royal Irish Academy, Dublin, 2005), p. 66.

9   *Irish Independent* (5 October 1914).

10   Clarke and Litton (1991), p. 51.

11   Ó Síocháin (2008), p. 277.

12   BMH WS 741, Michael J. Kehoe, p. 9.

13   Inglis (2002), p. 331.

14   Mac Lochlainn (2005), pp. 202–3.

BIBLIOGRAPHY

Andrews, C. S., *Dublin Made Me* (Lilliput Press, Dublin, 2001)

Augusteijn, J., *Patrick Pearse: The Making of a Revolutionary* (Palgrave Macmillan, London, 2010)

Barton, B., *The Secret Court Martial Records of the Easter Rising* (The History Press, Gloucestershire, 2010)

Brennan-Whitmore, W. J., *With the Irish in Frongoch* (Mercier Press, Cork, 2013)

Clare, A., *Unlikely Rebels: The Gifford Girls* (Mercier Press, Cork, 2011)

Clarke, K. (author) and Litton, H. (ed.), *Kathleen Clarke: Revolutionary Woman* (O'Brien Press, Dublin, 1991)

Clarke, T., *Glimpses of an Irish Felon's Prison Life* (Maunsel and Roberts, Dublin, 1922)

Connolly-O'Brien, N., *Portrait of a Rebel Father* (Talbot Press, Dublin, 1935)

Crowley, B., *Patrick Pearse: A Life in Pictures* (Mercier Press, Cork, 2013)

Curry, J., *Artist of the Revolution: The Cartoons of Ernest Kavanagh (1884–1916)* (Mercier Press, Cork, 2012)

Dudley Edwards, R., *Patrick Pearse: The Triumph of Failure* (Faber & Faber, London, 1977)

Dudley Edwards, R., *James Connolly* (Gill & Macmillan, Dublin, 1981)

Ferguson, S., *GPO Staff in 1916: Business as Usual* (Mercier Press, Cork, 2012)

Ferriter, D., *The Transformation of Ireland 1900–2000* (Profile Books, London, 2004)

Ferriter, D., *Judging Dev: A Reassessment of the Life and Legacy of Eamon de Valera* (Royal Irish Academy, Dublin, 2007)

FitzGerald, D., *Desmond's Rising: Memoirs 1913 to Easter 1916* (Liberties Press, Dublin, 2006)

Foy, M. T. and Barton, B., *The Easter Rising* (The History Press, Gloucestershire, 2011)

Gibney, J., *Seán Heuston: 16 Lives* (O'Brien Press, Dublin, 2013)

Gillis, L., *Revolution in Dublin: A Photographic History 1913–1923* (Mercier Press, Cork, 2013)

Good, J. (author) and Good, M. (ed.), *Enchanted by Dreams: The Journal of a Revolutionary* (Brandon Books, Dingle, 1996)

Greaves, C. D., *The Life and Times of James Connolly* (Lawrence and Wishart, London, 1986)

Hawkins, H., 'Joseph Conrad, Roger Casement and the Congo Reform Movement', *Journal of Modern Literature*, vol. 9, no. 1, 1981–2, p. 67

Henry, W., *Éamonn Ceannt: Supreme Sacrifice* (Mercier Press, Cork, 2012)

Higgins, R. and Uí Chollatáin, R. (eds), *The Life and After-life of P. H. Pearse* (Irish Academic Press, Dublin, 2009)

Hughes, B., *Michael Mallin: 16 Lives* (O'Brien Press, Dublin, 2012)

Inglis, B., *Roger Casement* (Penguin, London, 2002)

Jordan, A. J., *Major John MacBride 1865–68* (Westport Historical Society, Westport, 1991)

Laffan, M., 'The Making of a Revolutionary: Casement and the Volunteers, 1913–14', in Daly, M. (ed.), *Roger Casement in Irish and World History* (Royal Irish Academy, Dublin, 2005), pp. 64–73

Le Roux, L. N., *Tom Clarke and the Irish Freedom Movement* (Talbot Press, Dublin, 1936)

Litton, H., *Edward Daly: 16 Lives* (O'Brien Press, Dublin, 2013)

MacAtasney, G., *Seán Mac Diarmada: Mind of the Revolution* (Drumlin Publications, Manorhamilton, 2004)

MacAtasney, G., *Tom Clarke: Life, Liberty, Revolution* (Merrion, Dublin, 2012)

MacDonagh, T., 'Marching Song of the Irish Volunteers', *The Irish Review*, vol. 3, no. 34, December 1913, pp. 500–2

Mac Lochlainn, P. F., *Last Words: Letters and Statements of the Leaders Executed after the Rising at Easter 1916* (Government of Ireland, Dublin, 2005)

MacThomais, S., *Dead Interesting: Stories from the Graveyards of Dublin* (Mercier Press, Cork, 2012)

Matthews, A., *Renegades: Irish Republican Women 1900–1922* (Mercier Press, Cork, 2010)

Matthews, A., *The Kimmage Garrison, 1916: Making Billy-can Bombs at Larkfield* (Four Courts Press, Dublin, 2010)

McCracken, D. P., *MacBride's Brigade: Irish Commandoes in the Anglo-Boer War* (Four Courts Press, Dublin, 1999)

McGarry, F., *The Rising: Easter 1916* (Oxford University Press, Oxford, 2010)

McGough, E., *Diarmuid Lynch: A Forgotten Irish Patriot* (Mercier Press, Cork, 2013)

Mitchell, A., *Roger Casement: 16 Lives* (O'Brien Press, Dublin, 2013)

Nevin, D., *James Connolly: A Full Life* (Gill & Macmillan, Dublin, 2005)

Norstedt, J. A., *Thomas MacDonagh: A Critical Biography* (University of Virginia Press, Charlottesville, 1980)

O'Brien, P., *Uncommon Valour: 1916 and the Battle for the South Dublin Union* (Mercier Press, Cork, 2010)

O'Brien, P., *Crossfire: The Battle of the Four Courts, 1916* (New Island Books, Dublin, 2012)

Ó Brolcháin, H., *Joseph Plunkett: 16 Lives* (O'Brien Press, Dublin, 2012)

Ó Buachalla, S. (ed.), *A Significant Irish Educationalist: The Educational Writings of P. H. Pearse* (Mercier Press, Dublin and Cork, 1980)

Ó Comhraí, C., *Revolution in Connacht: A Photographic History 1913–1923* (Mercier Press, Cork, 2013)

Ó Conchubhair, B. (ed.), *Dublin's Fighting Story 1916–21* (Mercier Press, Cork, 2009)

Ó Conchubhair, B. (ed.), *Limerick's Fighting Story 1916–21* (Mercier Press, Cork, 2009)

Ó Conchubhair, B. (ed.), *Rebel Cork's Fighting Story 1916–21* (Mercier Press, Cork, 2009)

O'Farrell, M., *A Walk through Rebel Dublin* (Mercier Press, Cork, 1994)

O'Farrell, M., *50 Things You Didn't Know about 1916* (Mercier Press, Cork, 2009)

O'Farrell, M., *1916: What the People Saw* (Mercier Press, Cork, 2013)

O'Hanrahan, M., *Irish Heroines: Being a Lecture Written for and Delivered before An Árd Craobh Chumann na mBan, Dublin, during the Winter Preceding Easter Week, 1916* (O'Hanrahan family, Dublin, 1917)

O'Hanrahan, M., *When the Normans Came* (Browne & Nolan, Dublin, 1931)

Ó Ruairc, P., *Revolution: A Photographic History of Revolutionary Ireland 1913–1923* (Mercier Press, Cork, 2011)

Ó Síocháin, S., *Roger Casement: Imperialist, Rebel, Revolutionary* (Lilliput Press, Dublin, 2008)

Parks, E. W. and Parks, A. W., *Thomas MacDonagh: The Man, the Patriot, the Writer* (University of Georgia Press, Athens, 1967)

Pearse, M. B., *The Home Life of Padraig Pearse: As Told by Himself, His Family, His Friends* (Mercier Press, Dublin and Cork, 1979)

Pearse, P. Óg, *The Coming Revolution: The Political Writings and Speeches of Patrick Pearse* (Mercier Press, Cork, 2012)

Plunkett Dillon, G. (author) and Ó Brolcháin, H. (ed.), *All in the Blood: A Memoir of the Plunkett Family, the 1916 Rising and the War of Independence* (A&A Farmar, Dublin, 2006)

Reddin, K., 'A Man Called Pearse', *Studies*, vol. 34, no. 134, 1945, pp. 241–51

Ryan, D., *Remembering Sion: A Chronicle of Storm and Quiet* (Arthur Barker, London, 1934)

Sinn Féin Rebellion Handbook (The Weekly Irish Times, Dublin, 1917)

Sisson, E., *Pearse's Patriots: St Enda's and the Cult of Boyhood* (Cork University Press, Cork, 2004)

Stephens, J. (ed.), *The Poetical Works of Thomas MacDonagh* (T. Fisher Unwin Ltd, London, 1917)

Townshend, C., *Easter 1916: The Irish Rebellion* (Penguin, London, 2006)

Tracy, A., 'Michael O'Hanrahan', *Carloviana: The Journal of the Old Carlow Society*, December 1963, pp. 12–13, 38–9

Travers, Rev. C. J., 'Seán MacDiarmada 1883–1916', *Breifne: Journal of Cumann Seanchais Breifne*, vol. 3, no. 9, 1966, pp. 1–46

INDEX